BEHIND THE FACE

HOW RAPID CHANGE COMPELS BUSINESS TRANSFORMATION

Anil P Goel

INDIA · SINGAPORE · MALAYSIA

Notion Press

Old No. 38, New No. 6
McNichols Road, Chetpet
Chennai - 600 031

First Published by Notion Press 2018
Copyright © Anil P Goel 2018
All Rights Reserved.

ISBN

Paperback: 978-1-68466-455-9
Hardcase: 978-1-68466-908-0

For

Sneh Lata and the Late Kailash Chandra, my parents.

Contents

Foreword . . . . *ix*
Prologue . . . . *xiii*

1. From James Finlay to Tata Global Beverages **3**
   1. A Question of Balance. 3
   2. Munnar. 6
   3. Transformation 12
   4. Plantation Packed Freshness. 17
   5. Challenging the Status Quo 19
   6. Overseas Acquisitions. 23
   7. Employee Buyout 27
   8. The Global FMCG 31

2. The Taj's Journey over the Years **35**
   1. In Search of the Lost Chord. 35
   2. The Early Years 39
   3. Change of Guard in 1997 42
   4. The Baton Passes On 44
   5. The Perfect Storm. 48
   6. Setting the House in Order 50

3. Managing Change **57**
   1. Shifting Sands 57
   2. Mayhem in the Markets 59
   3. Shareholder/Lender Expectations 64
   4. Redefining the New Boom 65

4. Profit Improvement **69**
   1. Thinking Differently. 69
   2. Pricing 72
   3. Food and Beverage 77
   4. Manpower 79
   5. Reading the Barometer Right 81

5. Reforms Required **85**
   1. Shelter from the Storm 85
   2. Financing 86
   3. Taxation 88
   4. Construction 90
   5. Land 91

6. The Corner Room **95**
   1   The Voice 95
   2. Environment 99
   3. Sector Knowledge 102
   4. Value Creation 104
   5. People 106
   6. Customers 109

7. The Situation Room **115**
   1. Unplugged 115
   2. Business Strategy 118
   3. Fund-Raising and Capital Allocation 123
   4. The Art of Balance Sheet Management 127
   5. Operations 131
   6. Investors and Analysts 135
   7. Technology 141
   8. Grooming Future CFOs 146

8. The Board Room **151**
   1. Imagine 151
   2. Board Composition 154
   3. Board Committees 158
   4. Board Accountability and Independence 165
   5. Board Effectiveness 167

Acknowledgements *177*
References *181*

Nobody knows about what's going on
With the world and the steel,
The flesh and the bone
River keeps flowing and the grass still grows,
And the spirit keeps going, nobody knows
Poets they come and poets they go,
Politicians and preachers they all claim to know

– Allman Brothers Band –

Song: Nobody Knows. **Album:** An Evening with Allman Brothers Band.
Record label: Epic Records.

Foreword

Mask Behind The Face is full of nuggets and insights gleaned by the author from nearly four decades of working behind the face of the Tata group—a conglomerate that has challenged sacred theories of 'core competence' and confounded management gurus across the world by excelling in a host of industries as diverse from steel to software, automobiles, hospitality, plantations and beverages.

This book is both a worm's eye view and a helicopter perspective by someone who cut his teeth as a fresh finance recruit with the Tatas. Along the way the author helped shape some of the businesses from behind the scenes, overcoming and leading epochal challenges in the tea, coffee plantations and branded beverages that are global brands today. In addition, he also played a key role in the Indian Hotels Company, which is inarguably the forerunner of the hotel industry in India, owning and operating the iconic hospitality brand of Taj Hotels.

It's a fine book from a keen observer, who rose to become the Executive Director of Taj Group *of* Hotels and also the CFO of two great Tata companies. This riveting story, full of anecdotes from his experience in the Tata group will help finance professionals, CEOs and Board members navigate the high seas of business prone to 'future shock' and uncertainties. This is a great ringside view by the author who was often in the ring himself.

Captain Gopinath

Founder, Air Deccan
Author - *Simply Fly and You Cannot Miss This Flight*
September 5, 2018

Come gather 'round people
Where ever you roam
And admit that the waters
Around you have grown
And accept it that soon
You'll be drenched to the bone
If your time to you
Is worth savin'
Then you better start swimmin'
Or you will sink like a stone
For the times they are a-changin'

– Bob Dylan –

Song: The Times They are a Changin. **Album:** The Bootleg Series Volume I to III.
Record label: Columbia Records.

Prologue

In October 2016, I retired from my job as the Executive Director & CFO (Chief Financial Officer) of The Indian Hotels Company Ltd (The Taj Group *of* Hotels), after working for over 35 years with the Tata Group. During these years, I had the opportunity and privilege of working at Tata Global Beverages for around twenty years and with The Indian Hotels Company Ltd for another fifteen years. During the latter part of my career with the Tata Group, between the years 2000 and 2004, I was the CFO of Tata Global Beverages and subsequently moved on to be the Executive Director and CFO of The Taj Group *of* Hotels, a position that I held up to the time of my retirement.

This book is an endeavour to capture my experiences, thoughts, beliefs, and concerns on the business environment surrounding the corporate world and my conviction on the need for us to 'change' to remain relevant.

Business' success in the future will be dependent upon an organisation's ability to pre-empt the forces of change, and to reinvent itself continuously in an environment of ever-increasing competition and changing market dynamics with all their related pressures and pulls. Based on my thirty-five years with the Tata Group, this book focuses on just that: how some companies have succeeded in doing this while some are yet to cover this ground. As such, I set out the lessons learnt as my thoughts on how managers need to start looking at business from a different lens. Based on the essential of 'change' to remain 'relevant,' *Mask Behind the Face* provides insights that will help us become better managers and enable us to run successful businesses.

Mask Behind the Face is experiential business history, anecdotal, yet diagnostic and also prescriptive at times, based on my in-depth understanding of two great Tata Group companies, operating in varying fields.

The narrative covers the evolution of Tata Global Beverages and Indian Hotels Company, two jewels within the Tata Group fold. The book covers how over the last four decades, both have adapted to the ever-changing environment in pursuit of their respective strategic objectives, albeit with varying results. The diagnostic thus throws up the recognition that increasingly, many of the tools of the past that helped us succeed in running a business have to be discarded now, to succeed in the future. In the course of the narrative, I chart out the factors that play into success and others that can lead to failure, and more importantly, I emphasise the need of timely course correction and unambiguous accountability within an organisation for delivery of shareholders returns.

The required course correction in organisational culture extends to corporate governance too. Having served on several boards, and watched many others function, I realise the overwhelming need for enhancing accountability and governance, the importance of which cannot be overstated. Accordingly, I lay out a roadmap that redefines the roles of the CEOs, the CFOs as company boards in the emerging new order, that collectively are accountable to the shareholders and other stakeholders of the organisation to ensure its sustainable success. This remains enormously pertinent to India, today more than ever before.

As stated by Alvin Toffler four decades back, success in the future will depend upon an organisation's ability to continuously 'learn, unlearn and relearn.' Such a transformation will need to start from the top of the organisation, before we can expect it to percolate down the ladder.

In the course of writing this book, I have sought inspiration and leaned upon many of the rock 'n' roll legends, their music and lyrics, that have over the last forty-five years moulded my thinking, my beliefs, and in which I found solace and inspiration. I have always felt that there has been a considerable amount of philosophical insights in much of the past folk, rock 'n' roll and blues music. It is left to us to dive in, indulge, absorb and get enlightened by the genius of such music legends and see how we can adopt some of what they say, through their music, in the corporate world. It is rather an interesting coincidence that as I started work on this manuscript, Bob Dylan got nominated for the Nobel Prize for Literature for 2016.

I had given considerable thought to the potential title for this book and chose to name it, as I did, based upon a thought that came into my mind when I was still ideating on the content. The genesis of the name is based upon my interpretation of the human personality, which in a manner of speaking is like a 'mask'—deep-rooted, well-defined and firm. The human face could thus be interpreted to be a mask as we traditionally perceive the latter, as facial expressions can and do camouflage our true feelings and emotions and often display emotions that are not true to what we feel. The relevance of all this is that our true personality and the many emotions that we display or not disclose in the daily course of our lives influence our conduct and decision-making. In turn our resultant behaviour in the course of work influences the business that we run and its destiny.

July 14, 2018

If you don't know the way
If you can't see the wood for the trees
Taste the wine from the water
Well what should it matter,
To the fool or the dreamer!

– Moody Blues –

Song: Blue Guitar. **Album:** The Best of Moody Blues. **Record label:** Polydor.

From James Finlay to Tata Global Beverages

A Question of Balance

On April 1, 1982, I joined Tata Global Beverages (the erstwhile Tata-Finlay and Tata Tea, in that order), as an Internal Auditor, and with that began a 35-year professional association with the Tata Group. In those days, the company was very strongly influenced by James Finlay PLC, which was the original promoter and still the majority shareholder. Amongst its various other ventures, James Finlay had pioneered entry into the tea plantation business in India, Kenya, Sri Lanka, and elsewhere. The Glasgow headquartered company had entered India way back in the late nineteenth century and progressively set up tea plantations in Assam, Bengal, Kerala and Tamil Nadu.

When the job offer came in, I must admit, that I knew precious little about Tata Global Beverages as an organisation, barring what I could pick up through a page turn of the company's Annual Report for 1980. However, having attended school in Jamshedpur, all that interested me was that I was joining the 'House of Tatas,' and for me that was enough. The fact that the job was Cochin based, entailed a fair amount of travel up to the plantations and would, therefore, uproot me away from my comfort zone in Calcutta was no issue for me. The early sense of adventure and dealing with the unknown excited me.

The company handed over a train ticket to me booked in a two-tier sleeper coach, and I set off on a three-day train journey from Calcutta to Cochin. At the Howrah station, I recall that I had picked up a copy of James Michener's *The Drifters* for all of Rs. 10.10 paise, that kept me enthralled through what was otherwise a rather uneventful train journey. While I was to be based at the company's office at Cochin, I had been advised by the company that on arrival at Cochin I should head straight up to Munnar, the tea plantations in Kerala, as the internal audits for the new season needed to get underway. On reaching Cochin, one of my assistants met me and we drove across to freshen up at the Hotel Hakoba, a small boarding lodge that was located on the sea-facing Broadway, in Ernakulam, and thereafter we embarked upon the three-hour drive up to Munnar. This 16-room boarding lodge has withstood the test of time and still operates, standing across the road from the Taj Group's Gateway Hotel. We reached Munnar in the evening and I was accommodated by the company at the High Range Club, which would be my home, for months at a stretch, for the next three years or so.

The Beginning

The Tatas original foray into tea was a very small step that they took, by setting up a joint venture with James Finlay in 1964, through which they had made an entry into the domestic branded tea production and distribution business. Those were early days in this sector for the Tatas and they limited their market presence in branded tea to Andhra Pradesh, Karnataka and Tamil Nadu. Separately, the Tatas had also set up an export-oriented instant tea plant in Munnar for which the green leaf was being purchased from the neighbouring James Finlay tea estates. These were cautious, but well-measured steps taken by the Tatas as the domestic tea market was still strongly dominated by Lipton and Brooke Bond. The Tatas' limited presence in the tea business continued for a decade and a half until such time that Darbari Seth, one of JRD Tata's key aide took over as the Chairman of the company. Besides being the Chairman of Tata Global Beverages, Darbari Seth was also at that time the Chairman of Tata Chemicals, Tata Oil Mills and Rallis, besides being a Director of Tata Sons. With long flowing silver hair, I recall that Darbari Seth was rather fond of wearing beige safari suits, which were fashionable around that time. Despite his eminence and stature in the corporate world, Darbari chose to be driven around in a Maruti Suzuki 800 car, a reflection of his humility and commitment towards energy conservation. Though a technocrat, Darbari Seth had a good understanding of finance. The combination of these skill sets made him into one of the pioneering leaders within the Tata Group, who amongst others, helped the Tatas expand their footprint in India in the 1980s and 1990s. I recall that it was under his stewardship that both Tata Chemicals and Tata Global Beverages raised funding in the 1980s through partially convertible debentures i.e. a part of each debenture face value was converted into equity shares, at a premium. The instrument, when launched, was a rage in the stock markets in those days when the financial markets in India were still evolving.

Munnar

The Scotsmen had arrived in Munnar in Kerala, in the late 1800s, found the district suitable for tea cultivation and thus commenced with the clearing of the jungles and planting of tea in all earnest. By 1894, 26 estates in Munnar had been registered by Finlay Muir & Company, a subsidiary of James Finlay and active tea planting and cultivation was underway. The Scotsmen were busy planting tea and expanding their footprint at what was clearly a frenetic pace of 600 acres of tea planting per year, under inarguably very trying conditions. In due course, the company controlled over 8800 hectares under tea and an additional 8000 hectares under fuel in Munnar, besides additional hectares under tea, coffee and fuel in the neighbouring Annamalai district in Tamil Nadu.

Munnar is a small hill station, three hours east of Cochin by road and similarly around three hours west of Coimbatore. The town got its name from a Tamil word, which means three rivers, as it is located on the confluence of three mountain streams. The tea plantations in Munnar were spread across some 900 square kilometres, at an altitude ranging between 5000 feet and 7000 feet. A little-known fact about Munnar is that it boasts of Anaimudi, which, standing at 8841 feet above mean sea level, is the highest mountain peak in India, south of the Himalayas. Munnar also boasts of the Rajamallay-Eravikulam sanctuary, which is the habitat of the Nilgiri Thar, also known as the Ibex.

Life on the Tea Estates

In the 1980s, a career in the tea plantations was still a sought-after opportunity in the corporate world, notwithstanding the isolation, as the quality of life was good and all plantation companies took extra pains to ensure that the estate managers were well looked after, lived in huge fully furnished bungalows, had abundant company provided domestic help, and related facilities.

There was a strong corporate focus on social activities, sports, club life, and so on to ensure that individuals who picked up a career in the plantations, were kept busy at work and play, such that they did not miss the city life that they had left behind. With all the perquisites thrown in, the effective cost to the company made the job attractive enough for youngsters. Most entry-level recruitments were candidates with a public school background.

The social life in Munnar was centred around the High Range Club, built in 1909, which was the district's watering hole. The club offered pretty much all sports activities including golf, tennis, squash, cricket, rugby, and other games. The clubhouse had two bars, dining rooms, a library, accommodation, movie theatre, barber shop, billiards rooms, cards room, and a crèche. Executives in the district were encouraged to be socially active and during the dry weather, the weekends were all spent at the club by most families residing in the district. The annual inter-club sports meets were the highlights of the district's social calendar. Wednesday evenings were earmarked for movies, and the club committee made great efforts to screen recent Hollywood movies.

Like the Army, the tea plantations have been steeped in traditions that have passed down through generations with great pride. The club had two bars. The first bar was the 'Pinches Bar,' attached to the lounge, where the dress protocol was red tie and jacket on Saturday evenings and smart casuals on other evenings. The bar was named in honour of one of the district's erstwhile General Manager. The second bar was a 'Men's Only' bar that allowed guests in, in any attire, including shorts, field clothes, and so on. Needless to say, ladies were not allowed into this bar. The club had a great tradition, passed down since the turn of the nineteenth century, as per which any estate manager who had spent thirty uninterrupted years in Munnar, would on retirement, have the privilege of hanging his hat on the wall of the 'Men's Only' bar. On his farewell eve, all his erstwhile assistants would carry the retiring manager on their shoulders, lift him up to enable the latter to hang his hat up on the wall. And there it would be preserved, along with the hats of other retirees, for posterity. I still recall that the earliest bowler hat to go up on the wall belonged to a planter named A. W. John who resided in the district between 1894 and 1936!

Munnar, being on the Western Ghats bore the brunt of the southwest monsoon each year, that would hit the district with clockwork precision in the first week of June and the deluge would last well up to October. Monsoon rains in Munnar were intense and heavy. Certain estates like Kalaar and Kadalar had over the years received annual rainfall well more than Cherrapunjee, in the North East, which was still reported to be the wettest district in the country in geography textbooks. Munnar's monsoon months were dreary, cold, and foggy with howling winds and made work on the plantations difficult and restricted all socialising activities to indoors. Chundavurrai, Yellapatty, Chittavurrai and Kundaly were four tea estates tucked away in the Eastern corner of the district. Because of the inhospitable terrain, road communication between these estates with Munnar town would invariably get restricted for weeks on end, each year, during the monsoons.

Thus, the Finlays decided to set up another small club, with a bar, tennis courts and a golf course at Kundaly in 1917, such that the planters based on the four estates and their families would have their own watering hole, not just during the monsoons, but also as an option to avoid the long drive into town each weekend, if they so desired. The Kundaly Club had its own chequered history and traditions. The single most remarkable tradition that I can recall is that the club did not ever hire a full-time steward. Each of the four estate managers and their assistants had a key to the clubhouse as also to the bar cabinet. For decades, members kept a log book of consumption of liquor in the bar, in the spirit of trust and good faith, and were self-billed accordingly. The club had no catering facilities and thus the families residing in the district relied on 'potluck' whenever they grouped together. A remarkable legacy that the club had nursed over the decades was to preserve the 'visitors' book' that would be presented to VIP guests for their comments and signature. I recall seeing the names of the late John F. Kennedy Jr and late Jacqueline Onassis amongst the many distinguished guests that had visited the club over the years.

Normally the visiting internal auditors spent a week at each estate to undertake the annual internal audit. During such visits, the estate manager would host us for lunch at his bungalow, as the district was far-flung, and it was not practical for us to drive back to the club for lunch on working days. Such social visits exposed me to formal four-course sit-down meals with estate managers at their bungalows, silver cutlery, imported crockery, white-gloved butlers who addressed the managers as 'master,' liquid soap in bathrooms, and well-used fireplaces, and so on. The planters lived in a world of their own, very different from the urban environment one was used to. There were no televisions in the district those days nor easy access to telephones. Even the local newspapers arrived a day late, in the afternoons. However, back editions of British newspapers and tabloids like The Daily Mirror, The Telegraph, Punch magazine, and so on continued to be very popular and were widely circulated across the district.

Munnar had as yet not been invaded by tourists and was thus still very pristine, uncrowded and vehicles in the district were limited to company cars, by and large. The pioneering Scotsmen from James Finlay, perhaps, fell in love with Munnar as it so reminded them of home. With all its lakes, waterfalls, jungles, flora fauna and abundant wildlife, the district was an undiscovered paradise.

In the late nineteenth century, when the Scotsmen decided to plant their stake in the district and set up tea plantations in Munnar, which while being in Kerala was not easily accessible from the West, or from Cochin. Thus, the Scotsmen had been compelled to bring up labour from the east, from Coimbatore in Tamil Nadu, to help clear the jungles, and plant tea. Since all the labour that arrived in the district was Tamil speaking, perforce, the official working language for the

Scotsmen from James Finlay also became Tamil and they learnt to read and write Tamil to be in a position to communicate with the workforce and administer the district.

In due course, spoken and written knowledge of Tamil became mandatory for all non-Tamil speaking executives that joined the company and they had to pass two exams in the language, conducted by the company, to get permanency of service. Legend also has it that in the early years, life obviously would have been very difficult for the contract labour that was brought up by the planters from Coimbatore, to work on the plantations. Because of the rather difficult living conditions, the incidence of a regular exodus of labour out of the district was high. The Scotsmen thus decided to mint their own currency, which would be valid only locally within the district. This move forced the contract labour to stay on in the district and the high incidence of deserters waned. I recall that one of the rare coins, minted and used by James Finlay as currency in that era, was framed and kept on display in the room that I used as my office at the company's Regional Office at Munnar.

In a manner of speaking, the plantations were at the time administered in a style similar to the Army administration. The estate manager's word was law for all residents within the estate. Larger tea estates had Assistant Managers to support the estate managers. The Assistant Managers would either be a dedicated support to supervise the plantation activities, or alternatively, focus on production within the tea factories.

Strict discipline across each individual estate was a paramount necessity not just for the smooth conduct of business on the estate, but even more so for supervising the conduct of the workforce and their dependents during non-working hours across labour lines. The Assistant Managers too needed to be kept under tight discipline, required as a part of their own grooming, and more so to ensure that the entire management walked the talk. These were hot-blooded youngsters and at times extended isolation can drive towards irrational behaviour.

Accordingly, the Scotsmen had left behind a rather unique tool to reign in an Assistant Manager that stepped out of line by allowing the estate manager to 'gate' an errant assistant. Being 'gated' meant that the assistant was not permitted to leave the confines of the estate for any social activity for a predetermined period, that is, no visit to the clubs or social calls nor would he be allowed to entertain friends in his bungalow during the period concerned!

This practice survived and in fact flourished within the district until the Tatas took control over the company and Krishna Kumar issued instructions to the General Manager to discontinue 'gating' of Assistant Managers. By the late 1980s, Krishna Kumar had been elevated to the position of Managing Director and Darbari Seth had in the former a strong ally who understood and shared the latter's vision. A recruit through the Tata Administrative Services, Krishna Kumar rapidly rose through the Tata Group hierarchy in the 1990s, eventually making it onto the board of Tata Sons. The son of an officer in the Indian Police Service, Krishna Kumar is a very pious individual and a fierce Tata loyalist. Having since retired from his various executive board positions within the Tata Group, Krishna Kumar continues to be a Trustee of Tata Trusts.

Transformation

While the Finlays did a remarkable job in setting up the plantations in India and managing them under trying conditions for over nine decades, by the mid-1970s they were clearly losing interest in the Indian business. By then the regulatory environment had become restrictive and repatriation of profits out of India was becoming increasingly difficult for the Glasgow based company. The drop in commodity prices, increasing costs and stringent regulatory environment convinced the head office in Glasgow that in the long-term the business would not be profitable. Thus, James Finlay chose to divest and exit from India totally, and for Darbari Seth, this was an opportunity offered on a silver platter, and he grabbed it.

Thus, in early 1984, the Tata Group acquired the majority stake in Tata-Finlay from James Finlay and after that renamed the company as Tata Tea. Hereon, began a journey that changed the destiny of this company and made it what it is today. The company name was further changed to Tata Global Beverages in 2008, aligned with its changed business, product portfolio and vision for the future.

James Finlay to Tata Global Beverages

The Tatas took control of the company, now better known as Tata Tea and set about quietly implementing a long-term turnaround plan, backed up by a significant capital infusion. The plantation business is labour intensive; it is vulnerable to commodity play on auction prices, and it is also subject to vagaries of the weather and its impact on the crop. The industry, in those days, was also grappling with limited research and development, both in the fields and in tea manufacturing, besides being plagued with very high social costs.

Darbari Seth ably assisted by Krishna Kumar, went about the task of turning the company around. Systematically, the company began investing substantial funds to improve the infrastructure across the plantations in the labour lines, covering accommodation, drinking water, roads, crèches, medical facilities, electricity, and schooling for the workforce.

The quantum of investments committed by the company enabled it to upgrade the infrastructure across its four plantation districts to levels well over what was prescribed in the archaic Plantation Labour Act. The company set up the High Range School in Munnar, which welcomed into its fold not just children of the district's management staff but also that of the labour workforce as well. In Assam, the company set up a Referral Hospital at Chubwa, open to the larger community in the area at subsidised costs while simultaneously investing to expand and modernise the Central Hospital at Munnar as well.

In parallel, the company set up an empowered R&D department, reporting directly to the Managing Director, which would focus on improving field practices, labour productivity, bush yield, irrigation and bush health. Over a period of time, various investments were made across the board to improve the tea bush yields that included inter alia, irrigation, infilling, replacement planting, changes in the skiffing and pruning policy to enhance bush health, identification of healthier clones, and with all of that the company was able to significantly enhance its annual tea crop with pretty much the same workforce. In effect, the labour productivity rose and that enabled a higher variable element in the wages for the workforce in the aggregate, a win-win situation for all.

The next step initiated was to modernise the company's tea factories, which had become old and outdated in the Finlay era. Investments were also made towards modernising the withering troughs, rollers, dryers, CTC batteries, stoves, sifting rooms and the like, along with the company setting up a new state of the art orthodox tea manufacturing factory at Chundavurrai, in Munnar. The new factory, then, was the largest individual orthodox tea manufacturing factory in Southern India.

Thus, over the next five to six years, the company transformed itself from an aged plantation company to a modern, well equipped plantation company whose tea was once again commanding a premium pricing in the domestic tea auctions. Krishna Kumar was a hard taskmaster. While huge investments had been made across the tea plantations, the results needed to be delivered as well. Accordingly, each individual tea estate had been benchmarked with its closest competitive set for monitoring of tea crop yields per hectare and auction prices, tea grade –wise. With this new work culture coupled with intense pressure to perform, the social greetings amongst the planters soon changed from the traditional 'hello' to a mandatory inquiry on the tea crop harvested during the week and the prices realised in the preceding tea auctions.

I recall that once a monthly performance review meeting was underway at the Regional Office at Munnar, the headquarters of the South India Plantation Division of the company. The manager of the Periakanal Estate was under fire as his tea crop productivity for the period under review was lower than the neighbouring tea estate owned by Harrison Malayalam. Needless to say, this situation was quite unacceptable to Krishna Kumar. In the course of discussions, the estate manager meandered around for a while offering various excuses for his tea estate's underperformance and concluded his own defence by stating that his estate had evidenced rather heavy rains and high winds that had combined to adversely impact his crop. Krishna Kumar all this while listened to the manager rather patiently. When the latter finished with his explanations, Krishna Kumar retorted with "and I guess the Harrison Malayalam's manager put a tarpaulin over his tea estate to protect it from heavy rain and high winds?!" That was the last time we ever heard of wind direction, terrain and rainfall as excuses for underperformance in the plantations.

With the first wave of transformational reforms having been completed, Darbari was still not satisfied as he knew that no matter what he did to lift Tata Global Beverages name, there was no escape for the company from the risk of fluctuation in auction prices that continued to be influenced by global commodity supply and demand imbalance.

Global prices of tea were still influenced by the consumption patterns of the affluent western consumers and the crop forecast in other key tea production sources like China, Kenya, Sri Lanka, etc.

Strategic Investment in Sri Lanka

After having modernised all the tea production factories across its tea estates and having brought in the best agricultural practices in its field operations, the company started looking overseas to explore possibilities of expanding its footprint in new geographies. What followed was a joint venture in Sri Lanka in the nineties to acquire a significant stake in Watawalla Plantations that gave Tata Global Beverages the much-needed access not just to the Sri Lankan teas, but to palm oil as well.

Open Offer for Consolidated Coffee Ltd

Around the same time, Darbari Seth made, what is perhaps the first ever 'open offer' in India for any company to acquire a controlling stake in another listed company. The target was Consolidated Coffee Ltd, the largest integrated coffee plantation company in Asia with significant hectares of pepper and cardamom along with abundant reserves of timber as well. When asked by the media what the strategic intent behind the acquisition was, Darbari's candid response was, "We acquired the company because God does not make land anymore." The lateral expansion from tea plantations into coffee plantations was a very natural and logical corollary for Tata Global Beverages and with that done, it had consolidated its position as a dominant plantation company in South Asia with a strong foothold in tea and coffee plantations.

Gambit in Russia

The next move by the two was to establish Tata Global Beverages presence in Russia, a significant tea consuming market. With the foreign exchange reserves within the country at a low ebb, the Indian government was encouraging the domestic tea industry to enhance tea trade with Russia under the barter mechanism. Accordingly for the company, the approach thought of was to make a strategic investment in a small Russian tea plantation company that was located in Sochi, on the Black Sea coast, and to use that as the base for the launch of an Indo/Soviet tea blend that would be marketed and distributed within Russia. I recall that after a month of financial and technical evaluation and due diligence by the management team, of which I was a member, Darbari Seth and Krishna Kumar flew down to Sochi to review the work undertaken and evaluate the opportunity. By the time they arrived, the management team had been able to put together the due diligence report, recommendations and the business case. We had, however, not got anywhere close to structuring the contours of the proposed Joint Venture Agreement, if at all a deal was to go through. In the course of reviewing the due diligence work undertaken and realising that the terms of reference of the intended Joint Venture Agreement had not as yet been sketched, the draft of the same was dictated by Darbari Seth, while he was having breakfast, which I wrote down in longhand and typed later on. That was the draft document that was used to negotiate the transaction with the Russian company. Such was the man's genius.

The opportunity to get into an alliance with a Soviet tea company was great, but ahead of its time, as with Gorbachev's subsequent exit from power, the USSR disintegrated and the rouble went into a free fall, rendering all business plans infructuous. Further, the managers of Krasnodar Tea Company, the joint venture partners were still mentally burdened with the legacy of their country's socialistic past and struggled to understand 'margins and profits.' The joint venture, notwithstanding its great promise, had to fold up a couple of years later on account of ever-increasing regulatory and economic complications within the erstwhile USSR, which were beyond the control of Tata Global Beverages.

Plantation Packed Freshness

Having turned around the core plantation business spread across Assam, West Bengal, Kerala and Tamil Nadu, established a presence for the company in Sri Lanka and acquired a controlling stake in Consolidated Coffee, Darbari Seth and Krishna Kumar were still concerned that the plantation business continued to be vulnerable to the commodity cycle of tea auction prices, which were influenced by tea buyers. Producers had limited control over the realisation value for their produce as the tea auction prices were in the grip of large buyers and blenders of tea.

Thus, the next transformation that Darbari Seth and Krishna Kumar embarked upon was to bite the bullet and invest behind an aggressive expansion in the domestic value-added branded tea segment, notwithstanding the prevalent domination of Lipton and Brooke Bond in the country. Lipton and Brooke Bond were large buyers, blenders and marketers, albeit with limited or no presence in tea plantation ownership. Krishna Kumar came up with the novel idea of establishing tea blending and packaging factories within the plantations itself with the intention to launch a portfolio of brands nationally on the platform of 'fresh and plantation packed.'

Since Tata Global Beverages harvested its own produce, blended and packed immediately thereafter on the tea plantations itself, it saved several weeks managing the logistics of 'bush to cup' thereby ensuring that the packed teas arrived in the hands of the consumers fresher than that of competition. Thus, the unique product positioning and brand communication to consumers was that a Tata Global Beverages product reaches the consumer several weeks ahead of the competition's products and thus was invariably a fresher product.

The company launched its first plantation packed brand named 'Kanan Devan' packed at the Malkiparai Tea Estate in the Annamalais in the late 1980s and subsequently followed it up by a national launch of its flagship tea brand named 'Tata Tea' backed by multiple packaging and blending production facilities across its plantation divisions. The company's foray into the branded tea market was a resounding success and slowly it established its portfolio of brands pan-India, and gave the well-established Lipton and Brooke Bond a run for their money.

In due course, Lipton and Brooke Bond were acquired by Hindustan Unilever Ltd and that company was compelled to launch a new brand named *'Tazaa'* (which means 'fresh' in Hindi) to counter 'Tata Tea' and its unique freshness platform.

Over the next few years Tata Global Beverages consolidated its branded portfolio, set up a strong national logistics and distribution network and emerged as a leading national, branded tea player with a plantation background. Ownership of plantations was still a boon as it allowed Tata Global Beverages to access high-quality tea at a cost lower than the prices at which competition was accessing the same from the auctions and thus the company had a competitive advantage that was unique. Having established a pan-India FMCG distribution network, the company expanded its branded portfolio by launching branded cardamom, pepper, rice, coffee, and similar agro products. However, some of the non-tea brand launches met with an indifferent response from the market for a variety of reasons. Perhaps the company was still overtly tea focused and in my view this was an interesting opportunity that the company missed out on, through product diversification and leveraging its robust domestic retail distribution reach.

Nevertheless, once the domestic branded tea business had stabilised, the company initiated marketing of its homegrown brands in neighbouring countries that had a strong Indian diaspora.

The first significant phase of Tata Global Beverages successful transformation had been completed, as the organisation had consistently kept an eye on the external smoke signals and kept reengineering itself to remain combative.

Challenging the Status Quo

After a three-year stint in Internal Audit in 1985, I was transferred to the Corporate Finance Department of the company at Calcutta. I was quite enjoying my stint in finance, and Vaishali and I were married a year earlier. In a couple of years, Neha our daughter was born. My own career gradually progressed as well and I was looking at a long stint in Calcutta with the company and working my way up the hierarchy within the Corporate Finance Department. However, Krishna Kumar, who had seen my work in Internal Audit in the early days had other ideas and transferred me to the company's office at Cochin to oversee the financial activities of our South India sales and marketing office. The Cochin office handled the entire auction and brand, sales and marketing of the South India Plantations, commodity trading for the Spices Centre, instant tea exports along with overseeing the Export-Oriented Unit or the EOU that was set up in partnership with The Tetley Group of UK for manufacture of their brands to source their Polish market.

After a rather interesting three-year stint at Cochin, Krishna Kumar yet again convinced me to relocate to Munnar to now oversee the financial affairs of the South India Plantation Division. By then, the tea commodity markets had adversely turned, plantation wages had shot up, commodity prices were at rock bottom and all the benefits of the last decade's efforts had been eaten up by cost increases. The division was reeling and needed to be turned around.

After taking up my new job at Munnar, the first couple of weeks were devoted to setting up the systems and processes aligned to what I believed they ought to have been. Separately, I deputed an assistant to put together a repository of data and information estate-wise for the last ten years, such that data mining could commence for us to see below the layers on what had gone wrong and what needed to be done to remedy the situation and improve profitability.

What we did was not rocket science, as often business managers fail to see the obvious. Essentially our diagnostic revealed a very interesting trend. Of the twenty-nine tea estates in the division, including those in Tamil Nadu, there was a group of around fourteen tea estates that were inherently profitable. This group of estates had consistently high yields, efficient labour productivity, each had its own dedicated factory, production quality was good and the estates were able to command a premium in the tea auctions or alternately, get a high percentage of their produce diverted into blends for the brands and thus get a share of the brand margins. The most senior and experienced estate managers were invariably assigned to run these properties.

The second group of estates, seven in number, were marginal players. Their yields were lower and so was labour productivity. The fixed cost of cultivation per kg produced was high. This group was a classic reflection of the commodity play i.e. if auction prices were ruling high, the group would be profitable and conversely, if the auction prices declined, the group's margins would erode rapidly.

The third group of estates comprised substantially of tea estates that did not have their own individual factories and thus supplied their daily crop to neighbouring factories. For a variety of logical reasons, in a place like Munnar, where all the twenty-five tea estates were contiguous to each other, the management believed that it was not necessary to have production facilities across individual tea estates, but rather locate larger production facilities spread across fewer estates so that within them they have the capacity to manufacture the daily peak crop for the district.

Thus, we had a group of non-factory estates that were, by and large, staffed by first-time estate managers or Acting Managers. When the Scotsmen were running the district, they were allowed a three-and-a-half month furlough every three years such that they could take the steamer across to the UK for a holiday and meet family and friends. During this time, their property would be overseen by an Acting Manager, an executive who had as yet not received a permanent posting at an individual estate and would thus move around every four months filling in for somebody who was away on vacation. Very often, Acting Managers would be drawn from this pool of estates to fill in for those who were proceeding on long leave. In essence, the legacy practice had created an impression that the underperforming group of estates could not do better and those manning these properties viewed the posting as a temporary aberration, pending correction by transfer out to a better estate.

The first problem identified by us was that the underperforming third group of estates were over a period of time being treated as a training ground for Acting Managers and for want of 'ownership' and lack of 'continuity', such assets were consistently performing below potential. There was no accountability, ownership, desire or expectation to improve the situation.

The next problem and the fundamental issue was that the management had wilfully 'accepted' that this group of tea estates were laggards and incapable of performing better. The bar had thus been progressively lowered subconsciously and it was thought to be alright.

And finally, the management practices and agricultural policies for all these estates were centrally codified, with little room for the manager to take initiatives based upon his own reading of ground conditions. Over standardisation of agricultural practices and inflexibility in management policy had taken deep roots.

This was the fundamental malady that needed to be corrected. The need was for us to be aware of the changing environment and thus have the ability to 'unlearn' what is no longer relevant and after that 'relearn' as Toffler has talked about. It was time for the management to change the way they ran the plantations, break the shackles of past practices and be open-minded towards alternate points of view.

Further detailed drill down on per kg production costs, per hectare cultivation costs, trend analysis of auction price movement, namely the gap in sale price realisation for this group of estates nailed the hypothesis that the 'as is' needed to end and that a turnaround of this group, while possible, would call for a new thinking, changed agricultural practices and more importantly 'accountability' with 'authority' to make decisions. We could ill afford to allow a very significant percentage of the division's tea acreage to continue as perennial loss leaders and hide behind the better run properties. Clearly, there was enough evidence of significant assets not generating an economic return on capital employed.

Thus the bottom line of what we recommended to Krishna Kumar was to turn past beliefs and practices on its head by deputing our best men to man these estates, to turn them around, as against perennially allowing a musical chair of part-time managers floating in and out of the properties. Also, we recommended that the managers needed the flexibility to alter cultivation practices more suitable to the individual estate and to also be able to monitor and control the destiny of their produce. More importantly, management itself needed to recognise that we had allowed a group of our assets to underperform continuously over a period of time believing it was okay. It was no longer okay!

Krishna Kumar realised the merits of the detailed diagnostic that we presented along with a plan for remedial measures. Late T. V. Alexander, a bright Production Manager and a bit of a rebel, was handpicked by Krishna Kumar to take charge of the entire group of underperforming tea estates and Alexander was empowered with the freedom and authority to do whatever was needed to fix it all.

With this changed mindset and unshackling the legacy of the past, Alexander did a remarkable job in turning around the performance of the perennially underperforming tea estates. This, in turn, contributed to the company's South India Plantations once again reporting record production and profitability as each estate was being held accountable individually to deliver sustainable profitability and laggards were no longer allowed to hide behind better-performing estates. In due course, Alexander went on to become the Managing Director of Kanan Devan Hills Produce Company Ltd.

Overseas Acquisitions

The Tetley Group, the second largest global tea brand owned by UK based Allied Domecq, had interests in a variety of businesses, including beer, liquor, and such. Around 1994, Allied Domecq restructured their business and decided to exit from tea and The Tetley Group was put on the block. As soon as Krishna Kumar came to know of this, he saw in The Tetley Group a game-changing opportunity for Tata Global Beverages to morph itself once and for all into a global branded tea player.

While Tata Global Beverages had by then become the largest fully integrated tea plantation company in the world, the potential synergy with the Tetley portfolio offered immense opportunities. Tetley was the largest branded tea player in the United Kingdom and Canada by far, with a play in North Eastern USA, Australia, Poland, and some other countries as well. Unlike Tata Global Beverages, which focussed on delivering value-added tea in packets, Tetley was fully focussed on the high-end tea bag segment. Krishna Kumar believed that if he could get his hands on Tetley, the fusion of the two organisations along with the complementary strengths of each could create a truly global enterprise with immense potential. Darbari Seth bought in Krishna Kumar's vision and approved for Tata Global Beverages to throw its hat into the ring.

However, the financial markets in India were very different at that time. They had not evolved, and Indian corporates found it difficult to raise foreign currency financing. India's own foreign currency reserves at that time were wafer thin. Thus, Tata Global Beverages, despite all its efforts was unable to raise the required financing on time to make a credible bid within the prescribed timeline and was pipped at the post by Prudential and Schroder, Venture Capitalists who bought The Tetley Group.

For Tata Global Beverages it was an important learning and the bid process helped open up a relationship with the Tetley management.

This led to the formation of a small joint venture between the two organisations, which was set up at Cochin to produce Tetley tea bags for export to their Polish market and elsewhere.

With time, Krishna Kumar got elevated to the position of Vice Chairman of Tata Global Beverages and moved on to Mumbai taking over additional charge as the Managing Director of The Indian Hotels Company which ran the Taj Group of Hotels.

Sometime in 1999, the Venture Capitalist that had bought The Tetley Group decided to cash out and exit. Michael Oaten, a partner of the erstwhile Arthur Andersen, was aware of Tata's interest in Tetley and so shot off a letter to Syed Kidwai, the new Managing Director of Tata Global Beverages in Calcutta informing him of the re-emergence of the opportunity and enquiring about any renewed Tata interest in Tetley. Syed faxed that letter to Krishna Kumar letting him know that The Tetley Group was up for grabs once again.

It's an interesting coincidence, rather filmy I might add, that the day Michael Oaten's letter arrived in Krishna Kumar's office, that very afternoon Wouter Kolff, the global CEO of Rabo Bank was to make a courtesy call on Krishna Kumar. The former made a big pitch to him about Rabo's keen interest in India and a desire to work with the House of Tatas.

By then Darbari Seth had retired and Ratan Tata had taken over as Chairman of Tata Global Beverages. Armed with the knowledge of The Tetley Group being available once again and a preliminary but strong expression of interest by Rabo Bank to help finance any potential bid, Krishna Kumar had all that was required to seek approval from Ratan Tata, Noshir Soonawala, Finance Director of Tata Sons and the Tata Global Beverages Board, to go after The Tetley Group yet again.

In 1997, soon after Krishna Kumar took over as the Managing Director of The Indian Hotels Company, he transferred me from

Tata Global Beverages to Indian Hotels to help him set up the required financial, regulatory and governance compliance protocol across the Taj Group's companies. While I was busy with my new work at the Taj, because of my tea background, I got pulled into the Tetley acquisition-related work and assisted the Tata Global Beverages management in the negotiation of the Sale and Purchase Agreements, legal due diligence, and financing for the transaction.

In early 2000, Tata Global Beverages successfully completed the acquisition of The Tetley Group which was approximately a Pounds Sterling 271 million (US $ five hundred million) transaction, leveraged and by far the first cross-border acquisition by any Indian corporation. Then, the acquisition of an iconic British brand by an Indian entity was unheard of in that part of the world. The managers within The Tetley Group were quite naturally nervous and high strung as could be expected in the circumstances. Krishna Kumar was not insensitive to the dynamics of what was going on and had wisely 'locked in' the services of all the key managerial personnel within The Tetley Group for a pre-determined period to ensure that the boat was not rocked and there was continuity within the business. Once the deal had closed, Krishna Kumar flew to London to hold an open town hall meeting with The Tetley Group's managers as a much-needed icebreaker. Amongst the many things that he talked about, I am told that he had stated to the effect that "In this transaction, there is no victor nor a vanquished. This is a partnership between two great organisations; each with a rich legacy of pioneering work undertaken for over a century. The fusion of the two entities has given birth to a new force that aims to be a dominant player in the global tea arena. With the backing of the House of Tatas, Tetley's future is now very bright."

Soon after the transaction closed, it just so happened that the Late S Kabiraj, who was the Executive Director, Finance, of Tata Global Beverages at that time was scheduled to retire. It was then that Noshir Soonawala, Director, Finance, of Tata Sons offered me the opportunity to go back to Tata Global Beverages as the CFO, an offer that was a great honour, which I gladly accepted.

I was the CFO of Tata Global Beverages for four years between 2000 and 2004. Those were very exciting years for the company that was in the last phase of morphing itself into a truly global enterprise. While the key focus for us was to nurse the new acquisition—fuse the two organisations together in a seamless manner, bring about all the synergies, manage the varying cultural dynamics between the two organisations, and so on—for me the single largest issue was to manage the acquisition debt and ensure that Tetley generated the free cash flows as per the business plan. Thus it would be in a position to progressively retire its debt, without imposing any financial burden on Tata Global Beverages standalone Balance Sheet.

The acquisition debt had been raised through Rabo Bank, without recourse to Tata Global Beverages and thus the bank covenants were stringent. It took about two years for things to settle down and for the two businesses to get integrated operationally, while Tetley was allowed its independent legal status on account of the non-recourse debt. In year three, post the acquisition, the company found an opportunity to refinance the entire debt and in the process reduce the interest costs of The Tetley Group's debt by close to Pounds Sterling five million per annum for the future. With that behind us, the acquisition had stabilised and Tetley now had the headroom in its operating cash flows to recommence investing behind the brand and growth.

Employee Buyout

In a fifteen-year journey, by the year 2000, Tata Global Beverages had truly transformed itself, well beyond what one may have imagined for it in 1985 when the vision for this company's growth had crystallised. Closer to home, while the bouquet of brands in the company's stable continued to grow and flourish, the plantations were beginning to cause concern for the company yet again. The cost of the social overheads being incurred to run the plantations, stagnant yields, and the oscillating commodity prices at the domestic auctions were eroding profitability. What was once the strength of the company had now become a problem because of the ever-increasing gap between the cost of production versus auction prices. With a brand-driven front-end of the business, ownership of plantations was no longer a competitive advantage and thus no longer a necessity.

I have earlier in this narrative delved substantially upon the century-old legacy of the Munnar plantations that the Tatas inherited from James Finlay and the commitment of the former over the next three decades to transform the plantations into a self-funding sustainable business, notwithstanding cyclicality of commodity prices. In this regard, the Tatas left no stone unturned in their endeavour to make the company's plantations business not just financially successful but also as a platform to showcase the group's commitment towards corporate social responsibility, by continuous investments to improve the well-being of the company's 60,000 labour workforce and their dependents. Notwithstanding all the emotions and history, when it was time to recognise a change in approach, the House of Tatas did not hesitate to take a difficult call.

The Tatas and the company board recognised the new reality, based upon all the diagnostics presented by management and soon enough mandated the management to come up with a plan for the divestment of the company's South India Plantation Division, albeit with a rider that under the intended new structure, the workforce must not lose their jobs and livelihoods and should, in fact, become co-owners of the business. After all, the company was blessed with a resident loyal and fourth generation workforce, and their interests needed to be protected in any ownership restructure that was to be undertaken. This was yet again a reflection of the unconventional thinking among the Tatas. They were willing to let go of the very business that they had nurtured and nursed for over two decades recognising that future value lay under an alternate ownership model.

With the board's direction in hand, the management initially spent months to explore the possibility of carving out the plantations under the prevalent provisions of the Kerala State Co-operative Act. However, after months of effort and research, we realised that the archaic laws and norms as prescribed under the Kerala State Co-operative Act were too restrictive in nature to allow putting in place the transformational restructure that we had in mind.

The pressure to find a solution was building up, while the plantations profitability continued to get dented because of a variety of factors. It was at that time that I had a chance meeting with Nachiket Mor, Executive Director of ICICI Bank, who was focussing on the Bank's Corporate Social Responsibility or CSR initiative. Nachiket was bubbling with ideas and saw in the large rural plantation workforce of Tata Global Beverages a captive base that could be reached out for enabling an improvement in their livelihood. This meeting turned out to be a game changer as ICICI Bank was excited about what the company had in mind and wanted to partner Tata Global Beverages, as best as they could, to help us achieve our objectives in the transformation of our holdings in the plantations.

What thus the company put in place was the first ever 'employee buyout' in Corporate India as per which, the company carved out its South India Plantations Division and shifted the ownership thereof to the 30,000 employee workforce, who would collectively now own the plantations under the new company structure. ICICI Bank came in to finance the new entity to help it cut the umbilical cord with Tata Global Beverages and enable it to stand on its own feet—financially independent. The company funded the workforce through loans to enable them to buy the allocated shares in the new employee-owned entity.

The management team that was under Tata Global Beverages running the plantations all migrated to the new company as owner and management. The board of this new company invited a lady tea plucker, who consistently had the highest plucking average within the district, onto the board as a representative of the labour workforce. The new entity was named Kanan Devan Hills Produce Company Ltd. Tata Global Beverages, while retaining a significant minority stake in the company, allowed full autonomy to the new owners, while being available to mentor and support the leadership on arm's length. This was, without doubt, the first ever employee buyout in Indian corporate history.

Krishna Kumar appointed the Late T.V. Alexander as the new entity's first Managing Director. A smart choice, as the business transformation needed a maverick at its helm of affairs to shake things up and unleash the required reforms to turn things around. Alexander, given the free hand that he had, went about the task like a man possessed—he delayered the organisation, amalgamated the tea estates into larger entities for administrative ease, reconfigured the green leaf transfer within the district and tea manufacture facilities for logistical ease, introduced altered tea leaf skiffing cycles in order to improve plucking labour productivity and reduced administrative costs across the board. In short, his changed business model broke away from the legacy of the past and put Kanan Devan Hills Produce Company Ltd. on the path of sustainable profitability as a plantation company. It is now well over a decade since the formation of Kanan Devan Hills Produce Company Ltd.

Today Kanan Devan Hills Produce Company Ltd. continues to operate independently, profitably, under its unique avatar of majority ownership in the hands of its employees who also continue to manage the company. Indeed, the experiment was a resounding success.

In due course, the company divested a significant stake in its North India plantations as well, keeping the objectives above in mind.

The Global FMCG

Tata Global Beverages was now truly a global fast-moving consumer goods (FMCG) which was reflective in its new name. In 2004, after four years in the company as the CFO, I was yet again moved back to Indian Hotels Company, and now as the latter's new CFO.

In the subsequent years, Tata Global Beverages continued to grow from strength to strength. From an annual sales turnover of around Rs. 75 crores as was reported in 1981, the company had grown to touch an annual consolidated turnover of Rs. 7000 crores by the financial year ending March 31, 2018.

Clearly, the company has achieved a lot over the last four decades radically transforming itself from what it was in the mid-1980s to what it is now.

Tata Global Beverages has over a period of time morphed itself into the second largest player in branded tea in the world. Over 300 million servings of the company's various brands are consumed by its customers around the world daily. The company's portfolio of brands now includes Tata Tea, Tetley, Goodearth, Jemca, Eight O'Clock Coffee, Himalayan water, Tea Pigs, Tata Water plus, amongst others. In recent years the company also facilitated the entry of Starbucks coffee chain in India, through a joint venture with the latter. However, much more needs to be done by the company. Tata Global Beverages has a fabulous retail distribution network and a portfolio of brands that have a strong connection with its consumers. The company needs to embark upon the next cycle of organisational transformation, reinvigorate its portfolio of brands, pre-empt consumer needs as also competitive moves, to build on a new portfolio of product variants that will reduce its dependence on traditional black tea and thereby enable it to drive turnover, market share and enhanced profitability in the future.

Having said that, the success of Tata Global Beverages over the years was driven by clarity of vision and purpose. The organisation consistently could look into the future and think outside the box. More importantly, the organisation demonstrated the ability to execute transformational changes with time and under varying leadership and management styles. The organisation entered unchartered waters where it saw unaddressed opportunities and conversely it did not allow emotions nor ego to come in the way to exit businesses that were no longer relevant.

When I reflect back and think about the company as it was in 1982 when I joined it and its present avatar, what came to my mind was that iconic Virginia Slims advertisement with its timeless catchphrase:

"You've come a long way baby!"

Don't wait, don't wait
Don't wait for the good time to come
We got 'em right here, we're on the run
Don't wait, don't wait

— J J Cale —

Song: Don't Wait. **Album:** Any way the Wind Blows. **Record label:** Asylum Records.

The Taj's Journey over the Years

In Search of the Lost Chord

In July 2015, Rakesh Sarna, the erstwhile Chief Executive Officer (CEO) of the Taj Group *of* Hotels asked me to hold an interactive session for all our hotel General Managers and talk to them from the CFO's perspective on challenges that the company was facing, our strategy to address the same and thus the role that each of the hotel's General Managers needed to play, individually and collectively, to enable the company to meet its medium to long-term objectives. The intended offsite would include interactive sessions conducted by human resources, sales and marketing and operations as well. The program was designed to get all the hotel General Managers aligned to the company's new priorities and intent and thereby get them all on board. Rakesh Sarna, handpicked by Cyrus Mistry, the erstwhile Chairman of Tata Sons, had taken over as the CEO of the Taj Group of Hotels a year earlier, and not unexpectedly had embarked upon a series of organisational and management changes across the company.

Rakesh Sarna had been brought on board at a time when the Taj was gasping for air and the pain caused by unprecedented business pressure needed to be fixed quickly! The Taj had gone through a phase of making significant investments in the domestic and overseas market between 2005 to 2010 which, due to a variety of subsequent events, had left the company's Balance Sheet highly leveraged and profitability had declined. At the time, the company pursued its aggressive growth and when investment decisions were taken, the Taj was generating very strong operating cash flows and there was every reason for the company to believe that future cash from existing operations would continue to steadily improve, as the economic environment was strong. Thus, judicious increase in leverage was not a concern as the company believed it to be comfortably serviceable and within acceptable textbook tolerance.

The company had also recognised that the ongoing organic and inorganic growth in room inventory being pursued would need to be nursed through the normal gestation period before the new assets being added to the portfolio became cash accretive. However, the global economic meltdown in 2009 and its aftermath triggered an unprecedented pressure on the Taj, as also across the hospitality sector, leaving the company with high debt, a sudden decline in EBITDA, underperforming new assets, cost increases and eroding margins in the core domestic market itself. The subsequent events of 26/11 further added to the Taj's woes as its flagship hotel, the face of the brand and its cash cow was left significantly inoperational for a considerable period of time following the aftermath of the incident.

As is often the case with incoming new CEOs, Rakesh Sarna was in a hurry to start fixing things. The issues at hand that needed to be resolved were a first-time CEO's opportunity to make a visible and lasting mark quickly by doing the right things. The company was over-leveraged, significant investments made in some of the international markets had underperformed, a public bid to acquire an international chain of hotels had failed, the core domestic portfolio was eroding margins year after year and the company did not have the liquidity to modernise and renovate its flagship hotels in India.

In anticipation of a sustained economic boom in India, over the last decade, new hotel capacity in the country had grown in geometrical progression. Entrepreneurs with no hotelier background and real estate developers had diversified into investing in hotel assets and a plethora of international hotel chains had made a belated entry into the domestic market. Between the years 2004 to 2010, funding was accessible and leverage was 'kosher.' All this had triggered an unprecedented increase in the availability of new hotel rooms across the country at multiple price points.

With the slowdown in the economy after that, the unabated increase in all the new hotel capacity created an imbalance between the ever-increasing room supply in the market viz the demand for rooms. Such a gap gave the customers multiple choices and negotiating leverage. Major corporates were in any case also cutting back on expenditure, and arrivals of high spending international business travellers into India had declined. All of this combined to trigger a decline in hotel room rates significantly across markets, much to the bane of hotel companies.

Rakesh was a career Hyatt hotelier, with rich operational experience across the globe. He came in as a new CEO and inherited the legacy of a wonderful and iconic brand, a hotel portfolio comprising of many irreplaceable gems, a motivated workforce, strong customer loyalty, albeit with many inherent complexities and problems that required to be addressed quickly. Some of the Taj's flagship hotels were tired and needed to be renovated, the decline in profit margin had to be arrested and clearly, Rakesh would need to improve the performance of the company's US operations, which had become a big drain on its financial resources. He would also have to ensure that the company did not lose the license to operate the iconic Taj Man Singh hotel in Delhi (successfully retained by the Taj, pursuant to a public auction conducted by the New Delhi Municipal Corporation in September, 2018) and take a business call on the redevelopment of the Searock site in Mumbai with no further delay. Besides all this, he would need to nurse the Taj's relations with its various joint venture partners and other asset owners and grow the business in an asset-light manner, as also the margins. Problems aside, what Rakesh inherited was an organisation with a remarkably strong self-belief and work culture, the core of which was continuously centred around building and nursing 'relationships' with its customers, partners, associates and external stakeholders. Despite business related pressures, the rank and file of the organisation invariably displayed a high degree of passion to continuously 'delight it's guests' and steadfast commitment to the brand.

He had his work cut out.

Rakesh Sarna had been preceded as a CEO by Raymond Bickson, R K Krishna Kumar and Ajit Kerker, in that order. The Taj that Rakesh Sarna inherited was thus an organisation that was a broth of three diverse management styles, which had influenced the organisation over the last two decades. Since there were still many old timers in the organisation across levels, the influences of the past continued to linger on, many good and a few not so relevant at present and thus in need of change.

The Early Years

For a very long period leading up to 1997, the Taj was run by Ajit Kerker, under a strong regional organisational structure. Kerker started his career with the Taj Mahal hotel in Mumbai in the catering department and gradually worked his way up to become the CEO of the company when it was still a single hotel company. Over the years, with the help of an Initial Public Offering in 1970, Ajit started growing the company and established a footprint for the Taj to expand progressively across the country. More importantly, he brought in jewels like the Rambagh Palace, Lake Palace, and so on within the fold. In those days, the company was small and was undoubtedly the best in the league in India as it had some of the finest hotel General Managers in the business. Indeed that is the case even now. Across levels in the Taj, the staff continue to display an unparalleled commitment to the brand and sincere devotion to the guests.

The business in that era was administered and run under three regions and Ajit allowed each of the regional Chief Operating Officers (COOs) to run the business rather independently. Thus during the Ajit era, barring international operations, treasury, projects, hotel renovations and sales and marketing, most of the other functions including purchases were decentralised. The Taj Hotel's General Managers of that era were among the 'who's who' of the cities they were based in. Ajit Kerker's success as a hotelier was driven by his entrepreneurial bent of mind, early mover's advantage, risk-taking ability and a keen eye for detail on hotel designs, interiors and food and beverages. Anything that the Taj did was path-breaking, innovative and trendsetting.

Ajit succeeded in establishing a great brand also because, during his era, India as a market was still a protected economy and thus the domestic hospitality sector was limited to the presence of the Taj, the Oberoi, ITC and to a small extent, the Leela. The Indian market was still not considered to be of any significant importance by the international brands. Thus, Ajit succeeded in growing the business under the umbrella brand of Taj, irrespective of the hotel chain's individual product and price positioning across the domestic market. The Taj opened up unexplored markets like Kerala, Goa and Rajasthan, pioneered the introduction of international cuisine by opening trendsetting restaurants across the chain and perfected the art of consistently delivering warm Indian hospitality to its guests.

Besides opening up iconic hotels across the country, step by step, the Taj excelled in the introduction of memorable restaurants as well that include the likes of Shamiana, Zodiac Grill, House of Ming, Orient Express, Machaan, Handi, Golden Dragon, Thai Pavilion, and Trattoria, amongst others. Many restaurants of that era continue to flourish even now, well into the fourth decade of their existence.

The Zodiac Grill originally opened at the Taj Mahal Palace, Mumbai in the late 1980s. Such was the Taj's confidence in the impending success and acceptance of this new fine dining restaurant that in the initial weeks after opening, the restaurant's menu cards did not reflect any prices at all. The guests were encouraged to pay what they believed was the 'value' they saw in the entire dining experience. It is a matter of record now that in most cases, the guests tended to pay higher than what the restaurant would have otherwise charged for the meal.

While Ajit Kerker succeeded in India and ran a profitable business, his foray overseas was plagued by a combination of problems, including leveraged acquisitions, capital inadequacy, and an unclear brand positioning proposition. Even in those early days, the Taj saw the relevance of a selective international presence and progressively spread its footprint into Sri Lanka, Maldives, Dubai, Doha and after that into the United Kingdom and the United States. While the foray into the West was bold and well-intended, it did not add value to the brand visibility and the company bottom-line as the overall guest experience was a far cry from the elegance that the Taj was consistently providing across its Indian portfolio. Even in those early days, while the Taj's international foray met with fair success in the south Asian markets, the limitations of its brand pull were clearly exposed beyond South East Asia. Historically, the high-end domestic business for hotels within India originates from overseas and thus Ajit Kerker believed that the Taj must establish a presence within its key source markets, as also within markets its captive customers are going to.

Ajit Kerker did a wonderful job in expanding the company rapidly and positioning the Taj amongst the finest hospitality brands to emerge out of Asia. More importantly, the Taj provided to the Tata Group itself global visibility. Despite doing a lot of good, with time, some of Ajit Kerker's actions lead to a straining of relationships between the Taj and some of its significant asset partners, besides eventually with the House of Tatas itself.

Change of Guard in 1997

R.K. Krishna Kumar took over the reins from Kerker on the latter's exit from the business in 1997 and turned the company's organisational structure around by 180 degrees, which then was the right thing to do. Krishna Kumar dismantled the regional structure and consolidated control at the centre. The organisational leadership underwent a significant change, people left the business and new skills and talent were brought in.

While the business continued to be run under the Taj umbrella brand in the early days, the portfolio was carved out under well-defined internal Strategic Business Units or SBUs, styled as a luxury, business and leisure hotels to bring about customer centricity, consistent service standards and sharper product definition and positioning. Sales and Marketing function was strengthened with the formation of regional and international sales offices, customer loyalty programs were launched, purchases and IT were centralised, and executive compensation was improved along with a variety of reforms covering Human Resources.

Krishna Kumar decided to exit from the United States then, where the Taj owned and operated three-star properties in New York, Chicago and Washington as he did not want the Taj to be a 'me too' player. Importantly, Krishna Kumar cemented the Taj's relationships with the erstwhile royal families, some of whose palaces had been converted into luxury hotels by the Taj, and during the fag end of Kerker's reign such relationships had become strained. Similarly, Krishna Kumar also worked speedily to restore confidence among the various joint venture partners of the Taj Group.

Krishna Kumar took great pride in the Tata ownership and lineage of the Taj Group and gave visibility to the same in all external communication and brand promotions. In addition, the brand was revamped with new and refreshed logos, advertisements, media campaigns, and so on. The portfolio grew in the early days through

Mergers and Acquisitions (M&A) and some Greenfield projects. In particular, in those days the Taj opened new resorts in Goa, Jodhpur and Sri Lanka, built the Wellington Mews serviced apartments in Mumbai, acquired the Blue Diamond hotel in Pune, a hotel in Bandra, Mumbai now better known as Taj Lands End and entered into a joint venture with the GVK group of Hyderabad. The Taj also embarked upon a new cycle of selective renovations across the chain including the restoration of Falaknuma Palace in Hyderabad and St James in London.

There was a lot more that Krishna Kumar wanted to accomplish during his tenure as the CEO of the Taj Group. However, he was unfortunately handicapped in his pursuit of rapid growth of the business due to circumstances beyond his control, as the better part of his term was plagued by a series of global and regional events such as the events of 9/11, the Kargil war, severe acute respiratory syndrome or SARS, the foot and mouth scare and so on, all of which combined to adversely impact the fortunes of the hospitality sector. Thus, with pressure on profitability, the investments needed behind growth and renovations could not be deployed in line with the desired level and speed during his tenure as the CEO.

Krishna Kumar retired as the CEO in 2003.

The Baton Passes On

Raymond Bickson took over as the new CEO from Krishna Kumar. Raymond, a Hawaiian American was brought into the Taj by Ratan Tata to help bring about progressive globalisation in the Taj Group along with the introduction of best international practices. Before joining the Taj, Raymond had been the General Manager of The Mark, a 200-room hotel in New York. A very likeable person, fond of surfing, Raymond was a hotelier of repute, energetic and enthusiastic in everything he pursued. While Raymond took over as the new CEO, the company did, however, continue to have the benefit of Krishna Kumar's oversight on company strategy under the latter's new avatar as the Taj Group's Vice Chairman.

Raymond's entry coincided with the improvement in the economic environment, not just in India, but across the Taj's key overseas feeder markets as well. The improved profitability and the resultant strong cash flows helped the Taj pursue an aggressive growth plan, not just in India, but also in selective overseas markets once again. That was an era when the domestic market had begun opening up to the international chains which were queuing up for a presence in India by partnering with real estate developers and other first-time investors.

The thinking at the Taj then was for the company to continue to pursue growth in India across varying price points, while in the overseas markets, the Taj aspired to expand its presence selectively, but only at the high-end price point. Being a late entrant in the overseas markets, which were mature and dominated by well-established global brands, it was pointless for the Taj to be a 'me too' player.

The Taj also believed that investments in the overseas markets and making a financial success of the same, was important to enable the company to grow offshore through management contracts in the future, a model for growth that is capital light and facilitates speedy entry in the market. The continued thinking was not dramatically divorced from what it was in the Ajit Kerker's era, barring clarity on ensuring high-end brand positioning and unique locations within markets of choice. With time and with a dominant presence in India, the salience of the Taj's brand had widened as also the organisations own self-belief to make the brand a success in unchartered waters.

With the dramatic changes that were underway in the domestic markets such as entry of all significant global players, capacity expansion, and so on, the Taj now recognised that continuing to run the business under a global umbrella brand was no longer a sustainable solution. With time, the Taj's own portfolio had dramatically grown and the same was far too varied regarding product and service deliverables as were required to cater across varied markets, price points and customer profiles.

As a result, the Taj restructured its brand proposition by carving out a bulk of its existing hotels and rebranding them as either 'Vivanta by Taj' or 'The Gateway Hotel,' as the case might be. The privilege of carrying the Taj prefix was limited to only the luxury hotels within the portfolio. Each of the three brands now reflected a clearer product positioning, guest experience and a price point. Separately, the Taj had already launched its Ginger brand that was positioned at the hitherto unaddressed budget segment in the domestic market. In effect, the company had redefined itself into a multi-brand hotel chain that offered a high-end luxury experience under the Taj brand, five-star comforts under Vivanta by Taj, four-star offerings under The Gateway Hotels and the budget segment was addressed by the Ginger hotels.

This brand transformation was not divorced of complexities as all existing hotels would need to speedily align with their respective new brand positioning regarding product and service standards, customer experience, employee and asset owner orientation along with the need for a buy-in from external stakeholders, without diluting margins as a consequence of the rebranding.

While the brand architecture was undergoing a transformation, the company invested in acquiring iconic assets in New York, Boston, San Francisco, Sydney and Cape Town, while concurrently acquiring high-end leisure resorts for management in Seychelles, Mauritius, Marrakesh, etc. Simultaneously, the Taj pursued expansion in India as well and invested significantly in expanding the Vivanta by Taj brand. The growth of the Gateway brand was pursued almost entirely through management contracts.

Besides expansion of hotel room capacity, the company launched a new generation of restaurants across the chain that included the likes of Wasabi, Blue Ginger, Souk, Varq, and Masala, amongst others. Overseas, the Taj earned kudos for gastronomic excellence as the Quilon in London and the Campton Place Restaurant in San Francisco were bestowed with one star and two star Michelin ratings, respectively.

Things were going well and as per plan.

While all this was going on, the Taj's ambition to catapult itself into the global arena remained strong. It is at this juncture that the company made its now abortive open bid to acquire full ownership and control over the BVI based Belmond Ltd, the erstwhile Orient-Express Hotels Ltd, a boutique international hotel chain that also owned and ran the legendary Orient Express trains. Prior to making the bid, the company had acquired around 12 percent of the Belmond's traded stock from the open market in the belief that acquiring a significant stake in Belmond, and thereafter making an open bid for the rest of the listed shares would add credibility to the Taj's seriousness and add weight in the Taj's favour with the Belmond Board, whose support was critical in order to get any deal done. A fact not widely known is that the erstwhile promoter of Belmond had built a 'poison pill' around the listed shares of the company, whereby Belmond's Board controlled a majority vote of shareholders' resolutions through a 100 percent held subsidiary, and it could thus effectively block any bid on a possible change in the company ownership, if it so desired, without the need to refer the same to its shareholders.

From the Taj's perspective, acquisition of a boutique and reputable international brand was a desirable solution to establishing a global footprint, as against the alternative of a slow organic expansion of the homegrown brand across markets of strategic importance. The advantage of the former is that it facilitates speed to market, does not disrupt supply and brings in a captive customer base, albeit at a price premium. In the hotel industry, valuations of free-standing hotels too are often as expensive because of the underlying premium on real estate. Thus, if affordable, an acquisition of a branded chain was the preferred route. Then in 2009, the Taj had invested around US$ 262 million in acquiring the 12 percent equity stake in Belmond Hotels Ltd. Pursuant to two subsequent unsuccessful attempts to acquire that company, the Taj eventually divested the entire investment, albeit at a significant loss, as Belmond's own market capitalisation had subsequently declined significantly, largely on account of the company doubling its paid-up share capital in quick time coupled with a softening of the sentiments for the lodging sector in the United States. It was a bold and audacious move by the Taj, which unfortunately did not work for the company.

Aggressive growth that the company pursued between the years 2005 and 2010 resulted in a leveraging of the Balance Sheet, despite capital raising that was undertaken as some of the new assets acquired or invested in were not generating an economic return anywhere close to the original expectations. Cash flows were now under pressure and an urgent time-bound course correction was called for.

The Perfect Storm

As we all know, the perfect storm arrives without forewarning.

By 2009, the environment had dramatically changed. In the United States, with the scam on the collapse of the subprime mortgage market loans, the American housing market had crashed, the global financial markets were in disarray, the impact of which was widely felt around the world and soon enough percolated down to the domestic market in India as well and slowed down the hotel sector. The real pain, however, were the events of 26/11 on the company. It left the company with emotional, psychological and financial scars, which took a huge amount of subsequent effort to overcome.

How the Taj's hotel staff rose to the occasion, took care of their guests' safety at the cost of personal life is a matter of legend now and a well-documented fact. Ratan Tata and Krishna Kumar personally supervised the restoration of the hotel, the rehabilitation of the families of the deceased staff and speedily formed the Taj Public Service Welfare Trust to take care of the financial needs of those affected during the 26/11 attacks, not just within the Taj but also those across the city. The next of kin of the deceased hotel staff were extended the deceased employee's last drawn salary for the unexpired period of their respective service contracts, an unprecedented humane gesture displayed by Ratan Tata and Krishna Kumar. Decisions such as these have for decades enabled the Tata Group to stand out in the corporate world.

Despite all the trauma and psychological stress that was inflicted on the organisation and its staff by the events of 26/11, the company put all its resources and will together to partially reopen the lobby and the tower wing of the Taj Mahal hotel within three weeks of the traumatic incident. A solemn function was held to mark the occasion that was preceded by multi-faith prayer meetings. The Taj Mahal was back in business. That very evening, the board of directors of the company held an impromptu meeting to review the extent of damage to the hotel, probable restoration costs, restoration timelines and related matters.

The initial management thinking was to do everything possible to restore the palace wing and reopen it for business as early as possible. However, after deliberation Ratan Tata took the view, and rightly so, that the company needed to restore the heritage wing and all its restaurants and public areas back to their old glory, no holds barred. His view was that the budget for the restoration was not to be constrained by what the company hoped to recover from the insurer in due course. With that clear mandate duly supported by the board, it took the company around two years to restore and reopen the palace wing. These were indeed trying times for Taj.

The Taj management was being kept busy juggling with multiple balls in the air, while the sentiments for the hotel sector had weakened. In the aftermath of the global economic slump, coupled with the unprecedented increase in the availability of new rooms, the hospitality sector in India saw an overnight collapse by 20 percent in its pricing and the pricing has still not come back anywhere close to the peak of 2009! Conversely, during the subsequent years, the sector had been impacted by an unavoidable 5 to 6 percent cost escalation per annum, which had all combined to progressively erode margins in geometric progression.

Setting the House in Order

It was in this context that Rakesh Sarna took over as the new CEO in September 2014 on Raymond Bickson's departure from the company after a ten-year run as the CEO. One of the key changes that Rakesh Sarna wished to bring about in the way the company was run was to delink corporate supervision and control over the affairs of hotel operations while concurrently empowering individual hotel General Managers. He believed this would bring about a turnaround in the company operations and growth in profitability. Rakesh explained his approach as 'empowering but not abdicating!"

It was, to say the least, a rather unusual and high-risk move considering that all the complexities on hand were not resolvable at the individual hotel level. Dismantling of the Taj's national sales network and making the bulk of the sales force report to individual hotel General Managers was yet another questionable move. The Taj's strength in India was very clearly the strong relationships that had been built over the past many decades with its customers. These relationships were nursed centrally through the corporate sales office and the regional sales offices. Over the years, the Taj had, through this network, built the capability to market its wide portfolio through a single window discussion with a customer for any itinerary option across its chain of hotels. Such a core strength was wilfully unbuckled causing many eyebrows to be raised and strong protest from the sales and marketing team, besides others. Typically, individual hotels can be combative and can fight for business originating locally from within their respective market, relying upon brand pull, local sales support and the company website. However, there is just no way free-standing hotels can solicit and garner business from across their multiple feeder markets, concurrently, without the support of regional sales "feet on street." Any customer would expect a single window closure of enquiries and bookings, for an itinerary across a chain.

Similarly, the decision to reinstate the 'Taj' umbrella brand across the portfolio was a hurried decision and inadequately researched. With time, the Taj Group's hotel portfolio was far too varied and diverse, aligned to the market requirements, and it was too risky to take the portfolio back to 'umbrella branding,' where the company was a decade back.

Unrelated to these ongoings, before Rakesh took over as the CEO, I had already tabled a very comprehensive business restructuring plan to the Taj's board, embedded in which were potential solutions for addressing the Balance Sheet stress, mitigating asset impairment risks and facilitating debt reduction. The proposal entailed a combination of concurrent initiatives that included, inter alia, select asset divestments, shifting all the Taj's overseas investments into a single offshore apex 100 percent subsidiary and amalgamation/winding up of some of the subsidiaries, and so on. The combination of all of these, when undertaken, would reduce the leverage substantially and reinstate the dividend distribution ability of the company, and most importantly it would de-risk the profitability of the company from any future adverse impact of investment impairment.

This was accomplished by divestment of the company's hotels in Sydney and Boston, sale of the company's stake in Belmond along with divestment of some other non-core investments. Separately, through a complicated internal Balance Sheet restructuring, all of the company's investments in the various offshore assets hitherto held across multiple jurisdictions for legacy reasons, were shifted into a single directly held 100 percent offshore subsidiary named IHOCO NV (an acronym for Indian Hotels Company). This would enable the company to raise funds in the future in an optimal manner, with the value of its entire offshore business visible on a single Balance Sheet.

Under the implementation of this rather complicated business restructure, the high leverage had been substantially addressed.

From a peak consolidated debt of around Rs. 5200 crores on a Balance Sheet size of Rs. 9900 crores as it was in March 2015, the company had enabled a reduction of the consolidated debt down to around Rs. 3200 crores by September 2016, the point of my retirement.

With the Balance Sheet having been significantly addressed, the need of the hour for Rakesh was now to focus strongly on the company's operations and bring about solutions to improve the Taj Group's profits sustainably. The priorities clearly were to push for price leadership, refresh assets, strengthen customer loyalty, invest in digital platforms, and rationalise manpower costs. Most importantly, Rakesh needed to stem the cash losses from the company's US operations—a market that he knew exceedingly well. Above all, Rakesh would need to grow the business, reprioritise markets and ensure the appropriate return on investment, going forward.

While Rakesh Sarna had unleashed a variety of changes across the Taj, the consequences of which were gradually unfurling, in May, 2017 he announced his decision to quit the job, barely two and a half years into it. For the organisation this implied that Rakesh would not be around to take responsibility for his decisions during his short tenure and now the incoming Chief Executive Officer would need to freshly revaluate, yet again, many critical decisions of the past two years. Needless to say, the third change in a Chief Executive Officer, inside of three years has its consequences and the ability of the organisation to bear yet another course correction, in quick time, and hit the turf running would be tested. Time is of essence and the Taj would need to be nimble-footed. The combine of Marriot and Starwood hotels which had since taken over as the largest hotel chain in India would be testing the Taj's mettle in its own backyard.

Notwithstanding the prevalent competitive pressure, the resilience that the Taj has invariably displayed, the resolve of its people as also the strong connect that the brand has with its loyal customers will enable the company maintain its dominant position. The Taj is now poised to celebrate its 115th year of operations and will indeed grow from strength to strength.

And then one day you find,
Ten years have passed behind you
No one told you when to run,
You missed the starting gun.

— Pink Floyd—

Song: Time. **Album:** Dark side of the Moon. **Record label:** Harvest Records.

Managing Change

Shifting Sands

On October 14, 1981, an uncle of mine gifted me Alvin Toffler's *Future Shock*. I was 24 years old, had qualified as a Chartered Accountant and was working with Price Waterhouse & Co in Kolkata, as the firm was then known. I was aware of the book as it was popular while I was in college in the mid-1970s, but somehow I had not got my hands on it yet. Toffler's book left a lasting impression on me. I moved on to read Toffler's *The Third Wave* and *Power Shift* as well, subsequently.

I think, subconsciously and often knowingly, I leaned on Toffler's thinking, off and on in the course of my career, and sought inspiration to address problems and challenges that I encountered at work and to think through solutions. While Toffler wrote much of his work in the 1970s and early 1980s, his insights, diagnostics, implications of the ongoing change and advice was profound and is even more relevant today. What Toffler talked about has progressively unfurled and we have now witnessed. Toffler dealt with the overwhelming need for us to be 'future-ready,' as the pace with which technology and human behaviour were changing would leave society blindsided, as in his view, the 'future was overtaking us.' The change was underway and the pace thereof was escalating in geometric progression, disrupting social behaviour, conduct and impacting business.

Understanding the Forces of Change

Understanding 'change' is important because of the increasing irrelevance of the 'as is.' Nothing could be truer when you look at business and the multiple extraneous factors that impact and influence how we perform, our competitive edge, market share, margins, changing consumer behaviour and sustainable profitability. In the past, an entrepreneur required access to land, labour and capital to get started in business. Today, it is 'knowledge' that creates entrepreneurs. Knowledge is infinite, can be used concurrently by multiple people and can help be the differentiator that drives competitive advantage.

Winds of Change

Forty years ago, Toffler had predicted surrogate motherhood, the irrelevance of currency, information overload, missing supermarkets, diversity, paralysis of choices, online education, splintered families, the undisputed force of technology, and so on. Technology had made information available to all who cared and with that, the negotiating power had shifted away from manufacturers and service providers into the hands of consumers. In a short time, technology has and continues to dramatically change our lives. Technology, while creating opportunities was also causing severe disruption to the 'as is,' unknowingly to us and leaving us blindsided. Accordingly, the present state of affairs across the hospitality sector in India is so illustrative of the disruption caused by the unseen, silent yet brutal forces of change that continues to impact the business environment and the destiny of players in the market.

Mayhem in the Markets

Since 2010 the hospitality sector in India had been struggling due to a combination of oversupply of new hotel room capacity, a slowdown in the domestic economy as also across the key customer feeder markets into India, all of which coupled with the recurring cost-push inflation of at least 5 to 6 percent per annum had eroded the margins of all leading domestic hotel chains.

The problem had become further compounded as the first-time investors in hotel assets were sitting on high leverage on their Balance Sheets and were under pressure to service debt. Experience not being on their side, panic and short-sightedness set in, hotel room rates were allowed to get into a free fall in an endeavour to fill up the hotels. As we know, hotels have high operating leverage and continuous reduction in hotel room rates is not the desired answer to drive improved cash flows. The continued deep discounting in rates had triggered a bloodbath in the market; all were suffering and the customer was having the last laugh. Brands were getting commoditised! New York is by far the global nerve centre for the hospitality market and needless to say the competitive environment is fiercely combative. I recall that post 9/11, the hotel market in the city had tanked and demand weakened thereafter for several years. However, during that time, none of the top end brands in the city panicked and allowed a collapse in their daily room rates. These hotels held on to their pre 9/11 room rates, albeit allowing a decline in the room occupancies during the years of soft demand. Once the market strengthened again a few years down the line, the lead hotel chains in New York were able to push up their room rates in quick time to an all-time high. Conversely, those brands that allowed the room rates into a free fall, have struggled to catchup with the leaders in the pack.

The Taj was a victim of the mayhem in the marketplace as well and its own margins kept eroding as it could not insulate itself fully from the disarray in the market. All brands were busy looking over their shoulders and nobody was willing to break away from the herd and play a leadership role in the market. In this scenario, each new hotel that was opened in the domestic market, momentarily only added to the woes of the asset-owning companies as the operating cash flows from such new hotel inventory was invariably not strong enough in the initial years to absorb the cost of fixed operating overheads, interest and depreciation, and thus the pressure on profits only increased.

Desperate hope that the heady days of 2009 which the industry witnessed would return sometime soon was not going to help the cause.

Hope is not a great strategy.

Changing Market Dynamics

As the economy slowed down, while new hotel room supply inundated the market, the Taj could not insulate itself from all such external forces and the strong winds of change that had shifted the sands from beneath its very feet. The Taj's guests now had unprecedented choices and the internet provided them with information of supply, availability of rooms and pricing of all hotels in any market of their choice. Hoteliers now stood exposed, as never before.

To add to the industry's woes, online travel agents and Airbnbs of the world had caused unprecedented disruption in the industry by giving customers access to the free-standing unorganised hotels and accommodation across markets with online pricing information. Overnight, the size of the supply in the market had grown in geometric progression as all the free-standing unbranded hotels, motels, inns, guest houses as also B & B accommodation was now visible to travellers online and their option and choices had increased significantly, enabled by the recent entry of online hotel companies like Oyo in India, amongst others.

The cause of the hospitality sector was not helped by the significant recurrence of global and regional events that just did not allow any improvement in the situation. In the course of my career, I have always told investors and analysts that the hospitality business's fortunes are influenced by each day's headlines. Nothing could be truer as events since 2009 demonstrated. The economic meltdown of 2009, the LIBOR manipulation by several global banks, collapse of oil prices, weak European economy, a slowdown in China, and related events impaired whatever positive signs that were visible in India, post Narendra Modi's government being formed.

The Currency Play

In the past, hotel companies in India adopted a dual currency tariff according to which overseas visitors were quoted room rates in US dollars while domestic travellers were quoted tariffs in Indian rupees. In an era when the local currency gradually weakened, the US dollar tariffs had an inbuilt upside for the hoteliers regarding an ongoing currency gain benefit. In that era, the US dollar pegged room tariffs in India were invariably at a significant premium to the INR rates, with the latter applicable to domestic customers.

Some years ago, with the opening up of the economy and some pressure from the government, the hotel industry migrated to pricing their rooms only in Indian rupees for all customers, irrespective of nationality. This change coupled with the subsequent sharp fall in the rupee has significantly worked to the disadvantage for the sector insofar as overseas visitors are now paying for luxury rooms in equivalent US dollars, which is a fraction of what they paid in 2009. The good news, however, is that in this market, the industry is selling more hotel room nights across the country today than it ever did sell in the past! The demand for rooms thus continues to grow on an ever-expanding room supply base and the hotel companies now need to be smart about pricing and packaging the experience.

In my view, the trick lies in an ability to be in a position to segregate between fiercely loyal customers who are generally not very price sensitive. That segment of the business keeps coming in due to the brand's pull and assured service and stay experience. The next category of customers is those who would prefer a particular brand, other things being equal. This category is thus a bit price sensitive. Finally, the third category of customers is those who have limited brand affinity but are all the time fishing in the market for the best deal. For hoteliers, success lies in not treating the three categories of customers the same way and thus pricing the experience for each differently. This is, however, easier said than done. In a pricing free fall, the fiercely loyal repeat customers also benefit from unusually low pricing because pricing decisions driven by insecurity for business rub off across all customer categories.

Business Channels

In the new emerging order, armed with state of the art technology online travel agents have become giant aggregators, pushing the hotel tariffs downwards and in the process creaming off high double-digit margins at the cost of hotel chains. The cost of distribution for the hotel companies has gone up and the traditional sale forces are under immense pressure, as one-to-one customer relationships are presently contributing to lower business than was the case before. Aggregators presently hold the trump cards as they attract bookers and control large volume throughput.

Clearly, the customer has choices, as never before. Aggregators drive bulk bookings and keep pushing rates down; individual preferences have been subordinated. Most hotel chains have made a dash to strengthen their loyalty programs and are investing in upgrading their websites to increase direct business flows in an endeavour to reduce the cost of accessing business. However, much of this is too little too late.

Herd Mentality

A report issued by HVS India in September 2014 stated:

'India does not have a rate problem. If anything, we are just too afraid to charge a fair price for the product and service being offered, because the management feels that they will lose critical business unless they offer the lowest rates in town.'

The solution thus lies in hoteliers focussing in value creation for their guests through superlative service and stay experience as against just dropping the rates all the time.

The industry must thus realise that it cannot wait for a miracle to happen to improve its fortunes and profitability. The model on pricing and operating costs that worked until 2009 is not the solution for the future and the industry needs to reinvent itself in changing times.

Market Attractiveness

The long-term success of the hospitality sector is however contingent upon political stability within the markets in which it operates as that would favourably impact investment attractiveness. Also, such markets need to be seen as safe and tourist friendly. The combination of the two is essential for the sustainable success of destinations. This needs to be backed up by good accommodation and travel infrastructure, hygiene, safety and such other related factors that the industry needs to lobby for and work towards.

Shareholder/Lender Expectations

The question now is with all these complexities surrounding the business environment, how do we find the money to fund our business and invest for future growth? Shareholders are a patient lot. They own the businesses; the investment that they make in the company is unsecured and last in the hierarchy after secured and unsecured creditors. Thus, because they are patient and take high risks, their expectations of returns on investment are naturally high.

Lenders, on the other hand, play a different game. They finance businesses normally with security as a backup, on a pre-agreed return and repayment timelines, ring fence the operating cash flows to ensure that their debt is serviced. They would also lend unsecured, based upon the borrowers' goodwill and reputation, albeit for a higher yield.

Either way, irrespective of whether it's a shareholder investor or a lender, they expect performance and yield. The shareholders would measure economic return in the form of dividend yield on share price, growth in market capitalisation and ROI. They need to see a sustainable economic return on their investments, and beyond a point, management rhetoric on long-term and strategy does not fool anybody.

Redefining the New Boom

The trick thus was in us not waiting for the presumed turnaround of the economic conditions but to first believe in our minds that the buoyancy of 2009 was just a mirage. Let's pretend that the economic boom period of 2005 to 2009 never happened. If that be the case, we now need to convince ourselves that the environment as presently is actually the new boom period and even in these circumstances, we must learn how to run a flourishing business.

The challenge for us managers was to earn margins in 2018 in line with the healthy margins that the hotel industry earned before 2009.

Mantra for Success

There is a very interesting video of Roger Federer on YouTube, interacting with a bunch of bankers. In the short clip, Roger Federer talks about why and how he is, where he is and what he needs to keep doing to stay on the top of his game, as undoubtedly he is one of the best sportspersons in the world. In the video, Roger Federer talks about having a game plan, long-term and short-term structured goals, margins and the ability to change a plan if the going is not in line with expectations. Despite his unprecedented success, he talks about not resting on past successes but 'questions himself even during the good times.' Most importantly, Roger Federer talks about 'working on one's strengths such that he is always dangerous and unbeatable.

In my opinion, Roger's insights on how he plans ahead of each game and through the season to remain combative can teach us managers, a lot on how we can run our businesses more efficiently and stay on top of our game as well.

Approach to Creative Solutions

It's not easy to run a business and it's not meant to be. That's why we hire professional managers and pay them an attractive remuneration. The trick thus lies in an organisation's ability to grow, protect market share and generate sustainable profits, notwithstanding the external environment and changing influences. If the economic environment improves, the benefits are a windfall gain for which management should take no credit.

If as managers we accept the above, then, first of all, we need to recognise that we have a problem that we must address in a time-bound manner, diagnose the pain points, design solutions, have a desire to fix the problem, be accountable for action and thereafter execute the plan.

Everything thus begins by looking at one solution to move towards our business goals as against tabling ten reasons why we did not meet our targets, quarter after quarter.

If we take pride in what we do, no challenge is insurmountable and we can continue to create value for our shareholders, irrespective of the business environment. The key to running a well-grounded successful business is to pre-empt the winds of change and to keep adapting and innovating to counter the ever-changing conditions. What worked in the past is not necessarily a sustainable solution for the future.

As managers, we have an obligation towards our shareholders and other stakeholders to run the business in an ethical and sustainably profitable manner, irrespective of extraneous environment. That is our minimal obligation as professionals. In such a situation the need of the hour is agility, pre-emption and ongoing course correction.

Rejoice, rejoice

We have no choice

But, to carry on.

– Crosby, Stills and Nash –

Song: Carry On/Questions. **Album:** Carry On. **Record label:** Atlantic Records.

Profit Improvement

Thinking Differently

So where do we go from here? Enough has been said and written about the gloomy economic environment, the relative oversupply of new hotel capacity in the Indian domestic market, the competition snapping at each other's heels as if there is no tomorrow, and all the disruption being caused by online travel agents who are busy aggregating volumes, placing continuous pressure on pricing and thereby pushing the brands on to their knees. Such technology-driven disruption that forces a shift in the power from the hands of the manufacturer/service providers into the hands of distributors and retailers was talked about by Alvin Toffler in his book *Power Shift*, also written over three decades ago.

Toffler had explained that with the passage of time, technology would provide information, data and diagnostics that would enable insights into the consumer behavioural pattern, preferences and choices that in turn would facilitate departmental stores to decide what they need to store, in what volumes and how to display the same, as against manufacturers calling the shots as used to be the case in the past. This very same analogy applies not just to the hospitality sector but also to many other industries as well.

The hotel industry now needs to wake up to the new order and move to plan B as against continuing to labour in a state of denial. Getting caught blindsided is poor management and after that not doing anything about it is worse. The time has come to swiftly move to where the opportunities will be as against continuing to be stuck in an old and rigid mindset.

The biggest mistake managers most often make is to look at the performance of a profit centre from an elevated view, review its consolidated bottom-line inclusive of its various individual subsects of the operations, and be pleased with themselves if the number that they see is on target, better or close enough. Accordingly, in such a situation, opportunities for improvement or identification of problems simmering below the surface remain unaddressed. Managers often mechanically compare business performance with the previous quarter or year, and if we are ahead, it's great. If not, we have enough reasons to table for the same! We tend to take our eye away from the strong undercurrents that flow beneath the apparent calm water surface. It is, thus, always necessary to dig into the details to get all the facts right and thereby be in a position to take optimal and timely decisions bearing in mind that the headwinds will soon enough emerge and gain strength. I have always believed that it is easy to take tough decisions when the business is under pressure. After all, what choice does the management have, but to turn things around in quick time or perish? However, it is during the good times that smart organisations will devote time and resources towards innovation, product improvement, cost rationalisation, etc. to enable the organisation to be ever ready to face the changing dynamics of the marketplace.

The need of the hour is to challenge all legacy practices, costs, policies and what hoteliers loosely refer to as 'brand and guest standards' for product and service. The industry now needs to pause, question itself and drill down minutely into all elements of current pricing, fixed and variable costs to identify all the unknown and inadvertent value destruction that continues unabated largely across the industry. Conversely, opportunities unaddressed that go a-begging need to be addressed. In simple terms, hoteliers need to understand the effective price at which to sell each room for a night and concurrently also know the margin that accrues from each such transaction. In this business, fixed and variable costs continue to be incurred under the guise of 'necessary to maintain brand standards.' The industry needs to have brand standards for sustainable margins and profitability as well!

Dealing with Seasonality

Hotels, irrespective of geographical location or customer segmentation are not insulated from the impact on business on account of seasonality. This results in the sector being exposed to high operating leverage as fixed overheads are incurred, irrespective of occupancies and scale of ongoing business. During the off-season, it's difficult to cut back on much of such fixed overheads as all normal repairs, maintenance and renovations of guest areas are undertaken. By the time the busy season window opens, much of the annual costs have been incurred or committed to, with a little avenue for intervention in the event of business being weak during the subsequent peak season months.

Profit Centres

A good way to begin to address profit improvement opportunities is for the hotel General Manager to sit down with a blueprint of his hotel and to carve out the entire built-up area thereof into revenue-generating and non-revenue-generating areas. Typically, hotels generate revenue from rooms, restaurants, banqueting, business centres, spa and health clubs, retail outlet rentals, and so on. The bulk of the capital is invested across these areas. Back of the house areas are the operating nerve ends of a hotel and would include the kitchens, engineering, maintenance, stores, staff facilities which provide support to the front-end guest-facing areas. Accordingly, it is important for management to start focussing individually at each revenue-generating area's cost and profitability and through the process, margin improvement opportunities will spring up and be visible.

Running hotels can be an easy business if one is able to understand the inherent complexities of the business, and deal with them as a process and have a plan that addresses each commercial subsect within a hotel.

Pricing

A unique complexity of this business is the discomforting level of decentralisation that drives decisions on pricing and rate contracts. To my mind, this uniqueness can either be a significant game changer and advantage for the business regarding the speed of efficient decision-making or conversely can become the business' Achilles heel.

In most businesses that I am aware of, product pricing is traditionally a centrally driven decision whereby, at any point in time, for product-wise, stock keeping unit or SKU-wise, market-wise and month-wise list prices are decided and communicated to the sales offices and the field staff. The local deviation is not encouraged. Thus, for the sales staff, it's all about chasing and delivering the volumes in the sale at pre-determined prices.

Hotels differ in this regard as rate contracting, closing sale inquiries, accepting reservations and thereby committing the organisation to a transaction takes place at multiple points concurrently, 24X7 across the portfolio, through multiple booking offices. Typically, bookings flow into the funnel concurrently through centrally negotiated corporate contracts, website, hotel reservation offices, regional sales offices, call centres and so on. Pricing for any particular room category would also vary depending upon the multiple customer categories that include, among other things, national accounts, conferences, airlines, and fully independent traveller or FIT segment. To add to all these variables, an additional complexity relates to the 'inclusive' negotiated in the daily room rate, which could include in the quoted room rates the cost of breakfast, happy hours, laundry, Wi-Fi, airport pick-up, and so on.

This complicated pricing structure results in losing focus from the 'effective margin' that would accrue to the hotel from each room night that it sells, at any price point, relating to a particular customer segment. Managers subconsciously tend to get carried away by monitoring the turnover being booked as against concurrently looking at the quality of operating margin that the business booked will deliver. In all fairness, the insecurity to sell a room fast is also linked to the fact that a hotel room is a perishable commodity. If not sold for a particular date by a particular time, the revenue lost is gone forever.

Customer's Perspective

Let us begin with pricing. Hoteliers, thus, first of all, need to step back and relook at what they are doing from the lens of the customer and the guest. What this means is that for corporate clients, which are the bulk of the business for city hotels, for every room night sold, there are essentially two customers. The first is the individual checked in guest and the second is the employer organisation that settles the cheque.

In a recessionary market, where there is a pressure to cut back on hotel stay costs and the cost of the stay itself, hoteliers need to relook at all the 'inclusive' packaged in their gross pricing and other add-on facilities, in order to reduce the effective pricing in the hands of the customer, without diluting margins. Add-ons such as free breakfast, airport pick-up, unlimited Wi-Fi, laundry, a bottle of wine, flowers, chocolates, bottled water, and such items all add up to artificially pushing up the room rates and a hotel room night stay begins to look expensive in the eyes of the employer. The individual guest would rather stay in a hotel of his/her choice at a lower room rate, without many of the add-ons, as against getting shunted into an unattractive hotel by his/her employer as 'visually' the rate pricing of the latter appears much more competitive.

In India, for high-end hotels, around fifty-five percent of the annual business is presently driven by international arrivals, people who earn and pay in international currency and who normally visit India during the season months. In recent times, with the Indian Rupee having depreciated to around Rs. 74 to the US dollar, the fact of the matter is that for an individual spending in US dollars, India is a very cheap market; it always was, but even more so now.

Between 2010 to 2017, the average daily room rates in India, across the five-star deluxe hotels declined from US$ 205 to US$ 136. This collapse in the equivalent US$ room rates was on account of a decline in the daily rupee designated room rates themselves, which were further impacted negatively by the progressive strengthening of the US$ viz the Indian Rupee. (HVS Report 2017) That being the case, hoteliers in India need to think from the perspective of the US dollar spending guests. Such guests are not going to blink if they need to spend an additional US $10 on a daily room rate, but such a rate increase in tariffs, across its portfolio annually, can significantly improve a hotel company's profitability and long-term viability.

There is an art in ensuring that room rates do not continue in a free fall and conversely, rates actually commence to be pushed up subtly.

It's time for the hotel industry in India to relearn that art!

Hidden Costs

It's fashionable to benchmark ourselves with the best global practices and if that be the case, domestic hotel companies need to learn a few good practices from the large global chains. There is a huge amount of hidden cost that is incurred in extending early check in or late check out to guests rampantly. In an era when room rates and occupancies were high, it was fine in a selective manner.

However, in an environment of stagnant or declining rates and low profitability, hoteliers need to tighten up and avoid such unquantified hidden costs. The central issue here is that until 2009 when room rates were at an all-time high, a variety of facilities and add-on benefits were a part of the overall guest experience. Now with the rates being 20 percent behind peak rates of the past and costs having gone up by 30 percent over the record profit years, the price packaging of the past is no longer relevant. The model needs to change.

Margins from Long Stay Business

While hoteliers need to address the price mix to improve the quality of their margins, they must also keep an eye on the ball as far as customer volume mix is concerned. Typically, for city hotels, the weekend business is invariably at a low ebb as most guests would want to check out on Friday nights and will check in on Monday mornings. Thus, in a desire to sell room nights over the weekend and have an anchor customer base, hotels tend to bring in airline crew as these guests use hotels 24X7, seven days a week. However, this customer segment comes at the bottom of the price point. To add to the pricing woes, in recent times, hoteliers have started throwing in freebies into the airline crew pricing as well and thereby have made this customer segment pretty much a negative margin play. This needs to be corrected and would be possible if hoteliers learn the art of 'margin management' as against chasing top-line growth blindly.

Customer Segmentation

Rate negotiations with key corporate customers are typically undertaken in an annual cycle. The advantage of such an arrangement is that individual corporate contracts provide stable volumes per annum, pre-committed in lieu of which hotels agree to an annual rate, per hotel/ room category. This works well for corporates as well as it insulates them from the spike in room rates during the season months.

The meetings, conferences and events segment for city hotels is critical to help fill up the hotels and facilitate sold out dates and thus help spike up the rates in the shoulder dates surrounding such big events, besides contributing to the incremental banqueting business.

Eventually, the best pricing is secured by hotels from the fully independent traveller or FIT segment, which essentially comprises of non-contracted corporate business. This segment is the most lucrative for hotels, albeit with uncertainty surrounding the volumes stemming through this segment as demand crystallises at short notice.

Over the years, hotels have brought in the tool of revenue management to help strike a balance between room pricing and a volume push. Despite all the tools and technology backing them up to help bring in a scientific revenue management process within the system, the insecurity of losing the business has allowed a free fall in rates. I recall that once the CEO of one of the Taj's relationship bank phoned me and told me that he intended to hold his next board meeting at Bangalore and thus would need to host his bank's board of directors in one of the Taj's hotels within the city. I suggested a hotel that I believed would be convenient for this client's requirement and after that spoke to a colleague in sales to work up a rate offer. A few hours later, I received a rate proposal, which on scrutiny I felt to be rather defensive. I thus recommended an increase in the proposed room tariff by 15% and requested my colleague in sales to close the loop with the bank directly. The revised enhanced rate was calmly accepted by the bank, no to and fro negotiations took place and the business was sealed, to the satisfaction of all. The moral of the story is rather clear here! Have confidence in your product, service, brand pull and never allow the market to get even the slightest of a whiff of any insecurity to obtain the business.

It is evident that the art of revenue management in hotels is as yet in its infancy and there is much that the hospitality sector needs to learn from the airline industry on tariff optimisation. This calls for a change of mindset and confidence in the product and services that we sell.

Cost of Procuring Business

Lastly, hoteliers need to understand the cost at which business is procured across its multiple feeder channels. The commissions paid to the online travel agencies or OTAs, tour operators erode margins as variable costs as do the fixed costs of running in-house sales offices and call centres. In effect, the margin from each channel varies because the cost of procuring business varies and the trick lies in maximising business from channels that have the least variable cost per booking. More importantly, often, hotels do not have full visibility of commissions retained by travel agents as the sale is booked at the net rate received, after deduction of commissions. Such anomalies allow inefficiencies to breed within the system, as revenue that has leaked out of the system is not visible.

Food and Beverage

Hotels in India still drive a fair amount of business from in-house restaurants. Over a period of time, while free-standing restaurants have mushroomed across most metropolitan cities, high-end restaurants in hotels still do command patronage and premium in pricing. Needless to say, restaurants in hotels occupy valuable real estate, are capital intensive to set up, and thus need to be run as a business, with the hotel management looking at each individual restaurant and bar within a hotel as an independent profit centre.

The hotel industry has a tendency to over-invest in the restaurant's hardware in the belief that it will enhance the guest experience which in turn will drive business. Once again, looking from the perspective of the guest, a fine dining experience is all about great food, service and ambience. That is where the focus needs to be. The guest is least bothered about the brand of the table linen, wine glasses and that of the crockery and cutlery.

Restaurants need to be marketed as independent businesses and the General Managers need to ensure continued but elegant promotions, activities and celebrity sightings therein to keep the buzz going. The instances of failed restaurants within hotels must be reduced as far too much capital is invested in launching a new restaurant, besides the fact that it occupies valuable real estate. The restaurant chefs and managers must act as its brand managers and be visible and known to its patrons. With ever-increasing competition from free-standing restaurants in metropolis cities, the rules of the game have changed and the industry needs to adapt swiftly.

I recall an incident when I was entertaining some overseas visitors at the Wasabi in Taj Mahal, Mumbai. For one of the guests it was her second visit to the restaurant after a gap of a year or so. Once we had settled down at our table and the restaurant manager had exchanged pleasantries with the guests, he quietly changed the placement of the fork and the knife beside the lady's plate by shifting the knife to the left of the plate and the fork on the right thereof. The guest was left-handed, it's her second visit to the restaurant and the manager remembered! Such attention to detail is what makes the Taj stand apart and continue to delight its discerning guests.

Manpower

Another complexity of this business is the compulsion to deploy a large workforce across the hotels not just for guest service, but also for property maintenance and to deal with all the back of the house activities. Domestic hotel chains in India have typically deployed staff at levels more than what you would see in the western world for a hotel of similar size and configuration. With the cost of labour being relatively cheap in the past, hotels in India could well afford to deploy manpower rather liberally, which in turn allowed the Indian chains to provide unique and unparalleled service to their guests.

However, over the last decade or so, with the aspirations of the Indian middle class rising steadily and with the improved economic environment, the cost of hiring has been spiralling and has eroded margins. What was once the Indian hospitality sector's unique selling point or USP is now its bane.

So where do the solutions lie for the resurrection of the industry and for it to be able to pull itself out of the deep hole that it has dug for itself?

Hoteliers thus need to be sensitive to the overwhelming need to reduce the manpower deployed and the costs thereof. While there are no instant solutions, recognising that this is a big problem that needs to be addressed and having a desire to reflect over it is a good beginning. Typically, the deployment of manpower across a hotel would comprise of management staff, non-union supervisory staff, unionised staff, fixed-term contracted staff and outsourced labour. While the policy on management staff deployment and the cost thereof is influenced by the corporate office, the rest of the elements are pretty much in the hands and control of the hotel General Manager and his/her team.

It's now time for the hospitality sector to bring in the much-needed self-imposed discipline and to take the initiative for a time-bound series of reforms to bring about a reduction in headcount deployment.

With the ever-spiralling cost of manpower, a reduction in deployment is an overwhelming necessity for the industry to generate sustainable profitability and be viable over the long run. Often, the General Managers have a tendency to keep adding staff within the hotel in the belief that it is necessary to deliver the brand's service standards to the guests. I recall that many years ago, when Krishna Kumar was still the Managing Director and CEO of the Taj, in the course of a business review a discussion had opened up on the need to reduce the employee deployment and payroll costs and move towards multiskilling our workforce. An over-enthusiastic General Manager felt the compulsion to chip in and stated, "Sir, in my hotel we are now placing a spare bulb by the bedside so that just in case a lamp's bulb has fused, the guest can change the bulb without reaching out to housekeeping." Krishna Kumar's rebuttal was a quick "I thought we were discussing multiskilling our workforce and not our guests!"

The desired transformational change will need to be driven by the CEO as it calls for some logical but hard decisions. The required reforms will call for a freeze on recruitments, delayering, cutting back on staffing, aligning unionised staff costs to the competitive set in the market and a serious cut back in manpower sourced in a decentralised manner under fixed-term contracts and access to contracted labour through vendors. It is possible and necessary, but it needs a heart of steel to get it all done. It's better for the organisation to be lean and pay a premium above market to its workforce, as against allowing flab to accumulate and keep paying market linked compensation across the rank and file of its workforce.

Reading the Barometer Right

Senior leadership within the organisation must have the skills to be able to strike a balance between the multiple levers that drive a business, the importance and priorities for each, which will vary depending upon circumstances. More importantly, it is necessary for the organisational think tank to be in a position to look at operating parameters in the right context and not over-interpret any individual parameter in isolation. The need is for multiple and relevant cross-functional indicators to be reviewed concurrently, measure impact thereof and only after that arrive at conclusions.

There is no running away from the fact that successful businesses are those that can generate healthy cash flows and management is committed to that. Focus on sustainable cash flow drives profits, which in turn will ensure a healthy return on investment (ROI) above the cost of capital and thus ensure earnings per share (EPS) growth. Overindulgence in chasing improvement in isolated performance matrix can be dangerous if the organisation does not keep connecting all the dots to ensure that at the end of it all, the efforts are delivering shareholder value.

Thus, just chasing revenue growth is no good if the focus has shifted away from the quality of margins stemming from the business. Similarly, hoteliers have the inclination to over-rely on RevPAR (revenue per available rooms) as a barometer to measure own performance versus competition. While relevant and important, this criterion is helpful to compare similar sized hotels only and can mislead if over-relied upon. The point is that small capacity hotels competing at a prescribed positioning and price point must actually have a significant RevPAR premium over any larger capacity completion, as the former is easier to fill, irrespective of market conditions.

Most hotels conduct customer satisfaction surveys regularly. While this is a well-established industry practice, to make the effort meaningful, it's important to ensure that the response measured and being reported upon is from a credible sample size and the questions asked relate to parameters that drive towards customer retention and profitable growth.

The Human Resources team loves to undertake annual employee satisfaction surveys and the operations feel the compulsion to measure the Net Promoter Scores for their hotels to assess customer engagement with the brand. All this is fine and required, but the CEO should not view the outcome of each such criterion in isolation. At the end of the day, all these parameters must lead towards sustainable profitability and all the dots need to connect and point in the same desired direction.

While I have illustrated opportunities for improving business efficiencies in the context of the Indian hospitality sector, in my view, the approach is generic and cuts across sectors. All entrepreneurs and business leaders must pay granular attention to drilled down profit centre performance, customer segmentation, cost of sourcing business, margins, people costs and productivity and the like. Continuously challenging the 'as is' is the key to survival over the long-term.

Think Like an Owner

An organisational focus on long-term value creation and sustainable profitability will keep the shareholders supportive and happy. Concurrently, the organisation will have the financial wherewithal to invest behind an engaged and motivated workforce, happy customers and other stakeholders. Organisations will be successful if managers start thinking like owners. Certain misconceptions regarding perceived business value drivers will need to be dispelled such that the business' health check is continuously diagnosed right.

Instead of looking at short-term goals and thus avoiding inconvenience, CEOs will need to pick this up as their own key result area and drive the charge from the front. It's not enough to indulge in rhetoric, have grandiose plans, delegate it all and hope it all works and falls in place.

Last thing I remember, I was
Running for the door
I had to find the passage back
To the place
I was before
"Relax," said the night man
"We are programmed to receive.
You can check out any time you like,
But you can never leave"

– Eagles –

Song: Hotel California. **Album:** The Very Best of Eagles.
Record label: Warner Music Group.

Reforms Required

Shelter from the Storm

The Indian hospitality sector has tremendous potential to substantially improve its profitability sustainably, through a combination of internal discipline within the industry coupled with some relevant much-needed reforms in government policy, procedures and practices presently governing the sector.

The industry in India, as also around the rest of the world, is capital intensive, has long gestation periods and is labour intensive as well. Over and above the preceding, the unavoidable seasonality of business exposes the industry to high operating leverage and related risks. Conversely, however, the industry benefits on account of the longevity of hotel assets a relatively slower pace of obsolescence and is thus suitable for investors with a heart of steel and wherewithal to dig in for the long haul.

The crying need of the hour is for the government to recognise the contribution that the Indian hospitality sector makes to the economy as an employment generator, the significant indirect taxpayer, foreign currency generator, and so on for which the administration needs to look at this business through a different lens. This industry is not, by any standard, a non-priority lifestyle business! The reality is that notwithstanding the sluggish global economic environment, the travel and tourism industry continues to grow, across global markets, at a fair clip and has tremendous long-term prospects. However, one needs to survive the short terms to invest and plan towards the long-term.

Financing

The first reform that is long overdue is for the government to extend to the hospitality sector the status of an 'infrastructure industry.' This has been a crying need and a demand for the last two decades but the merit of the request has not been appreciated. The industry is not asking for nor expecting tax sops and subsidies. Being ascribed the status of 'infrastructure' would allow investors and hotel companies to access long-term funding, which is critical for the sustainable financial health of the industry.

Presently, hotel companies and promoters have access to only plain vanilla debt financing which typically would need to be fully repaid by the borrower, within seven to eight years from disbursement. Such debt instruments have limited or non-material moratorium periods towards principal repayment. Thus, essentially, the dysfunctional debt financing that is imposed upon the sector compels the borrowers to commence not just interest servicing but also debt repayment while new hotel projects are still in their infancy or at times when even construction is as yet not complete.

Even post commissioning of new projects, because of the nature of the industry, and notwithstanding the brand pull, any new hotel will take two to three years to stabilise its operations in any given market. If one assumes a minimum of four years to construct a new hotel in the Indian environment coupled with another two to three years to stabilise operations post opening, borrowers are presently compelled to commence retiring construction financing or refinance the same well before the new asset commences, generating steady cash flows. This unnecessary hurdle forces the industry into an avoidable black hole, stress refinancing and panic-driven short-term decisions. This is more so for first-time hotel project promoters who do not have the benefit of steady cash flows from existing and mature alternate hotel assets. This is one of the reasons that the domestic market has been inundated with ailing Greenfield projects in recent years.

If the sector is allowed to access long-term financing, with a moratorium on debt repayment for the first four years, such an intervention will minimise the abundance of unfinished or distressed assets that are presently struggling for survival in the market. After all, it's in the government's interest too to see investments fructify into cash-generating assets that trigger employment and revenue for the exchequer through incremental and recurring direct and indirect tax payments.

Taxation

In India, the sector is by far one of the most highly taxed industries, besides still being regulated by a variety of sector-specific, dated and archaic laws. Just to illustrate, the industry has been plagued by a variety of sector-specific additional taxes such as entertainment tax and luxury tax on its rooms and food and beverage billing, besides sales tax and excise duty on operational expenses. In addition, hotels need liquor licenses to operate bars, bartenders need annual licenses and daily banquet functions need prior liquor license on a day-to-day basis for each such venue!

The excise laws applicable to the sector are dated and draconian. Liquor stocks are still required to be kept in bonded stores under the supervision of excise officials, daily receipts and issues are supervised and recorded in excise registers and inventory issued for consumption for a function within the hotel cannot be brought back to the stores, if not fully consumed, and thus needs to be drained out!

The sector has invariably been adversely impacted by the old mindset and the ever-increasing 'moral police' who have their own point of view on when a bar may or may not be allowed to operate in a city or whether a city or state needs to go dry. One must also take into account the unquantified investments already made by the industry, organised and unorganised, that are now vulnerable to significant asset impairment because of continuous flip and flop in policy.

Luxury tax and entertainment tax rates have varied from state to state and many states have levied a luxury tax on hotel rooms rates based upon 'rack' rates published and not on the actual room tariff that the guest is eventually billed. Since the rack rates are merely a communication of brand positioning and intent, most often, actual rates at which rooms' business is transacted by hotels on a day-to-day basis are much lower. This is a rather unusual case of tax being levied on a value unlinked to actual revenue earned! It was expected that some of this would get addressed with the introduction of the much-anticipated Goods and Services Tax (GST) in India which became effective from July 2017.

Notwithstanding the foregoing, with the new tax rate being pegged @ 28% for room tariffs above a threshold rate as also on the food and beverages income, the effective new tax has brought no joy for the industry. Much more clearly needs to be done to address the burden of the overwhelming indirect tax regime that hounds this sector which invariably continues to be taxed at the high-end of the spectrum. This aberration relating to levy of tax on room rack rates is belatedly expected to be set right based upon an amendment to the GST norms as announced by the government in July 2018 whereby it intends to finally peg the tax on actual room tariff as against the notional rack rate.

A new problem encountered in recent years across multiple cities is the aggressive demands by local authorities towards property tax, linked to arbitrary changes in the formulae and rates that determined property valuation and the related annual tax thereon. Litigation and any appeal to reason have limited relief as the courts compel 50 percent of the demand to be deposited in court before an appeal being filed. Many city regulators have endeavoured to amend property tax related laws to change the formula and effectively recover, annually, a manifold increase in taxes from the assessees. This is an unusual situation as merely pushing up the rateable value of an asset does not improve its ability to generate cash!

Construction

Another legacy practice that continues to govern the destiny of the sector is the plethora of pre and post construction permits that a builder requires before commencing construction in any city in India and similarly separate approvals that are needed before a fully finished hotel being allowed to commence its commercial operations.

The process of securing pre and post building approvals is tedious, time-consuming, repetitive, expensive and most importantly adds to a huge time delay and resultant additional costs for project execution. While the process is painful, across cities, the nature of approvals does vary from city to city. In Maharashtra, the construction approvals required need to be secured from authorities as varied as The Pollution Control Board, Airport Authorities of India, Environmental clearances, Fire compliance approvals, Tree authority, Sewerage department, and so on. Most such departments are ill-equipped to handle the job and no sense of urgency is displayed at any quarter to review and process the applications on merit.

Needless to say, there is an overwhelming need for reforms relating to review and control over-processing of pre and post construction approvals for new hotel projects in India.

Land

Like others, the hotel industry also needs to bring in a greater discipline at their end in ensuring the financial viability of new projects against which capital is being committed. This would begin with ensuring an optimum debt/equity balance. Land acquisition is an expensive business and would need to be funded essentially out of equity. More importantly, the industry needs to ensure a balance between the land acquisition cost and the intended construction costs for the project. With time and increased demand, land valuation has been spiralling unabated and appears to be recession proof. Resultantly, the land value composition in the overall project cost has been mounting, across greenfield developments, testing the viability of many such projects.

The problem in the sector, and this spreads across geographies, is the ever-increasing disconnect between the perceived value of a hotel asset in the hands of investors and that asset's capability to generate sustainable cash from operations.

Over the years, hotel assets have been valued repeatedly at unviable turnover and/or EBITDA multiples for reasons that are not necessarily financially logical. Increasingly, there is a segregation between asset owners who do not manage hotels viz hotel managing companies that also own hotels. Accordingly, investors have surfaced who shop for trophy assets at any given EBITDA multiple, so long as they believe that the concerned asset will gain in its intrinsic real estate valuation in the future. Thus, hotel assets have increasingly become a tradable commodity, with valuations continuously being pushed up as there are invariably a few wise men who believe that there is a buck to be made at a higher price point, and thus operating cash flows from the underlying asset need not be the key guiding barometer for such investors. This is where financiers and lenders need to come in and play a role of responsible lending.

In conclusion, the pundits will need to realign their thinking to a whole new approach, relearn the art of attracting investments, and facilitating economic growth by removing many of the impediments that can be addressed without impacting the exchequer adversely. On its part, the industry itself needs to change its mindset, be nimble-footed, discard irrelevant legacy practices, and relearn the new skills for running a profitable business in an ever-changing environment.

This leads into the next section of this book in which I discuss the roles of the Chief Executive Officers, the Chief Financial Officers and the Board of Directors themselves, and how they need to be collectively held accountable and responsible to the shareholders for delivering sustainable financial health of the company that they are entrusted with.

It's funny how people just won't accept change

As if nature itself-they'd prefer rearranged

So hard to move on

When you are down in a hole

Where there is so little chance,

To experience the soul

— George Harrison —

Song: The Light that has Lighted the World. **Album:** Living in the Material World.
Record label: Apple Records.

The Corner Room

The Voice

In the course of my career, I have had the opportunity to see a dozen-odd CEOs at work, across companies and sectors. Such individuals ran the businesses at varying points of the economic cycles, regulatory and competitive environment over the last four decades. Needless to say, during the early part of my career, my exposure to the CEOs who ran the businesses that I was associated with was limited and distanced. The perceptions that I thus carry of such individuals is based upon my understanding and recall of how the business performed in those days and the outcome of decisions that they took. Clearly, I was not privy to the decision-making process nor the diagnostics that would have influenced strategic calls.

In due course, as my own career progressed and I moved up to the higher echelon of the company, I was progressively exposed to the corner room and all its intrigue. During that time, I was also exposed to the inner workings of listed and unlisted boards, eventually becoming a whole time Director and CFO myself and enjoying the privilege of chairing some of the Taj Group's companies. Over time, I have had the honour and privilege of working with some great minds.

Clearly, all the CEOs, as they progressively took charge were not in the same league. But all were CEOs nevertheless, and at the helm of affairs of ever-growing organisations grappling with ever-increasing complexities. Interestingly, when I reflect on the individuals that I had the privilege to work for or observe from a distance, I am unable to piece together a common thread in their personalities, skill set, professional background, management style, and so on.

The question that begs an answer is what makes a great CEO and how does a board select an individual to be a CEO in the first place? A great functional track record as a CXO or a corporate executive is not an assurance that at the next level the individual will excel as a CEO. We have all heard of the "Peter's Principle". At times in the corporate world, great CEOs are not perceived to have left a rich legacy of success and value creation behind, and conversely, average CEOs could come out looking dynamic because the economic environment just happened to be very favourable and business flourished, notwithstanding the individual.

The hallmark of a successful CEO would thus, in my view, stretch well beyond the financial results of the enterprise during the individual's tenure. What would count even more is the legacy that the individual leaves behind, that his/her successor wilfully builds upon, nourishes and strengthens while adding layers thereto of his/her own based upon the changing environment and marketplace.

The key issue here, thus, would be a CEO's impact on the DNA of an organisation. Nothing can be more traumatic for an organisation but to witness an upheaval within, each time a new CEO takes over. In effect, my experience tells me that there are no clear answers or trusted standards that govern CEO selection. There are, of course, the well-tested qualities any board would seek in any CEO candidate— high integrity, blazing professional track record, thinker, industry knowledge, etc. Despite all these well-established criteria, many CEOs meet with just moderate success or fail. Conversely, at times, untested CXOs have gone on to be successful.

Among the many 'must have' leadership qualities and skills for a successful CEO, which are the few that must form the common denominator? There are neither clear answers nor a prescribed formula that defines the qualities of great CEOs!

In the late seventies/very early eighties, I was wrapping up my degree in Chartered Accountancy in Calcutta and was on the threshold of embarking upon a career in the corporate world. Those days, Calcutta was still a 'happening city'. Most large multinational companies were headquartered in Calcutta, the clubs were buzzing and were accessible to corporate nominees for membership, cost of living was lower than Mumbai /Delhi while the quality of life offered by the city was good.

Some of the prized jobs for freshers, at the time, were offered by companies such as Dunlop, Metal Box, Guest Keen Williams, Union Carbide, Shaw Wallace, Remington Rand, and so on. Over a period of time, these companies have all got marginalised.

It's quite a story really and merits a great degree of thought and introspection on how, former great companies and market leaders, with operations cutting across multiple sectors, can wither away in quick time, if the leadership of the organisation has not kept an eagle eye on the dynamics of changing environment and the future at all times.

There are a variety of reasons on account of which businesses that are perceived to be dominant in the market and successfully run, buckle in unexpectedly at short notice. The malady begins with the organisation slipping into a comfort zone while resting on past laurels. In such instances, the key players within the organisation tend to herd towards the well-performing parts of the business and new initiatives in sunrise businesses tend to get neglected. People have a tendency to move away from risky new initiatives as it impacts assured performance incentives. It's ironical really because it's the new initiatives and investments for the future that need the CEO and his leadership team's quality attention consistently.

The solution lies with the recognition that as we grow the business and enter unchartered waters, the organisation itself would need to progressively undergo a change in mindset and needs to acquire new and incremental skills. Businesses often fail as the CEO is at times doing too much and losing focus or conversely not doing enough to safeguard the future. Symptoms of such a malady are visible if only one cares to see. A decline in the organisation's health is visible the moment the pace of its past profitable growth decelerates. This is followed by stagnation in performance for a few quarters, which leads to a recurring decline and eventually a collapse in profitability. The boards need to wake up the moment an organisation slips into the 'stagnant profits' stage.

It is in this context that I believe that CEOs need to display certain 'must have' skills and talent in an understanding of the environment, value creation, sector knowledge, customers and people. A good blend of these five, with thorough knowledge and awareness of each, will not only allow a CEO to succeed but more importantly, these skills are also necessary for the organisation itself to flourish and grow over the long-term.

Environment

The days of protected markets are over and well behind us. Increasingly, global influences are impacting our lives across markets and local governments have little control over such ongoing seismic shifts. As a result, corporations are often caught on the wrong foot because of the impact on their businesses, due to extraneous influences.

In some form or the other, either directly or indirectly, global influences are beginning to impact corporate bottom-line and in turn will influence an organisation's medium to long-term strategic plans on growth, capital allocation and investments. More importantly, an organisation's long-term health and survival are now dependent upon multiple extraneous influences and the ability of its CEO to continuously pre-empt and course correct.

To begin with, CEOs need to be well versed with the present government policy and with impending changes as they can have a significant impact. In economies such as that of India, government policy can change merely due to a change in a policy-maker, even in an environment where the same political party continues to be in power. Such a complexity percolates down to the state level as well, as there can be a total contrarian view on a subject matter between the position of the Centre and that of a State.

The regulatory environment is increasingly getting tightened and governance protocol is becoming ever so stringent. CEOs need to have more than a basic knowledge of regulations that govern corporate conduct, reporting and compliances.

Over a period of time, the INR has significantly weakened against most key currencies and in recent years the INR versus the US$ has been very volatile. Indian corporates are thus exposed to a new risk, which is presently managed by the CFOs but needs to be better understood by CEOs too. Irrespective of the health of its local Balance Sheet, it is becoming increasingly difficult for Indian corporates to support their non-INR offshore subsidiary companies on the strength of the parent company's INR Balance Sheet.

The volatility in the INR/US$ has pushed up the cost of borrowing for corporates locally, as the INR depreciation against the US$ has made foreign currency borrowing almost as expensive as traditional INR debt, once the cost of a currency hedge and FX depreciation is factored in.

That aside, there is the unaddressed exposure of the INR fluctuation against multiple currencies that Indian corporates running global businesses are exposed to and its impact on the quarterly Profit and Loss accounts. Such currency volatility benefits neither an exporter nor an importer, as nobody wants an open position and all are compelled to cover their exposures and are thus often caught blindsided.

The oscillation in the price of oil in recent years has been baffling, notwithstanding the additional shale oil and renewable energy production, a slowdown in the global economy and reduced global consumption. A swing between a low of $35 to a high of $120 per barrel is unexplained, notwithstanding geopolitical tensions. The effect of such price swings, a reflection of uncertain global forces, can be devastating for oil producing economies as also for consuming nations. Oil is after all one of the most mature industries, heavily researched and studied over the decades. Surely, by now the pundits need to have documented enough data on global consumption patterns, tapped reserves and untapped reserves, cost of production across source markets, quality of reserves, stock on the high seas, and such other factors. What then drives this mad oscillation in prices other than speculation and at times irrational behaviour? Sudden spurts in oil prices would impact the rupee to US dollar parity, trigger a cost-push inflationary pressure, amongst multiple other consequences domestically.

Enough has been said and written about the pace at which change in technology is offering opportunities while concurrently causing disruption in business. CEOs need to devote time to study the impact of technology changes in their businesses and get the organisations ready to pre-empt such headwinds.

Finally, while running global businesses, CEO strategy is now impacted by the dynamics of the ever-changing geopolitical scenario. The full impact of BREXIT on the UK and European markets is as yet unknown as the pull out timings continue to be uncertain. The outcome of the pullout will impact all businesses that supply to, or source from, or manufacture in Europe. Of late, United States, the largest economy in the world is threatening to become insular, inward-looking, resort to protectionism and impose restrictions on free flow of skilled labour.

In some form or the other, directly or indirectly, such shifting sands will impact business, its health and longevity, will call for pre-emption and course correction and CEOs will need to be on top of such issues to monitor and understand the impact of the same in their markets, their customers and implications thereof on the long-term viability and sustenance of their business.

Sector Knowledge

Once an individual occupies the corner office, it is critical for the incumbent to invest time to understand the business much better and in particular across functional verticals that he or she was not exposed to when his/her focus was on pursuing and delivering functional excellence. An all-round knowledge of sourcing, manufacture, quality, logistic, retail, and customers is critical for a CEO to be able to take balanced decisions, and more importantly, to be in a position to question and challenge the recommendations of the CXOs in order to be able to strike an optimal balance in decision-making and the outcome thereof.

I have always believed that the pace at which the environment is changing is so dramatic that no good practice or process is any longer good enough beyond the medium-term. One needs to keep challenging the 'as is' to find a better, cost-effective alternative. Such a transformation needs to be personally driven by the CEO, with conviction. This would be possible with the incumbent acquiring more than just the basic working knowledge across functions to be able to connect all the dots. The best way to go around this is to ask, question and continuously challenge the status quo.

There is a need to keep an eye on which way the business is heading, based upon the best diagnostic taking into account all known parameters. An eye on the next three-year forecast trends is a conversation the CEO needs to have with his CFO periodically. Knowledge and intelligence on competition, products, customer behavioural pattern, and a strategy on margin protection is required.

To be effective, CEOs will need to know where the money is invested in the business and where the profits are accruing from. While nursing the cash cows, the trick to lasting success is to make sure that new investments are nursed through the gestation period towards the desired profitability.

The worst mistake a CEO can make is to allow loss leaders to accumulate under his feet, camouflaged behind and supported by the cash cows. The risk to the organisation is that if we allow loss leaders and/or perennially underperforming assets to be stuck in a status quo, valuable resources get diverted away from the needs of the anchor assets and cash cows of the business. That would be a recipe for disaster.

Sector knowledge and in-depth knowledge of the organisation will help a CEO protect its competitive advantage. With time, unique selling propositions amongst the multiple players in a market become increasingly fuzzy. CEOs must thus have the wherewithal to be able to identify new competitive differentiators and build upon them, as entry barriers keep collapsing and competition heats up. The trick thus lies in a leader's ability to continuously re-engineer the organisation such that it can retain its competitive edge and remain relevant. Successful CEOs are those who can rapidly go beyond their own functional specialisation and speedily gain a firm grasp of the pillars that support the organisation. Continuous product innovation, identification of unaddressed opportunities in the market, striving for cost leadership, strong connection with the employees and customer centricity will enable CEOs to lead the organisation towards sustainable growth and profitability, irrespective of economic environment.

Value Creation

CEOs need to be committed to delivering sustainable value creation for the shareholders and thereby for its customers, vendors, employees and society at large. I do believe that if a CEO is focussed on driving value for shareholders ethically and responsibly, all constituents benefit. There, thus, needs to be clarity in the mind of a CEO on what is the matrix to measure shareholder value creation that can be consistently measured, monitored and reported externally and internally.

It's here that CEOs ought to reach out to their CFOs for guidance and assistance to work out the organisation's roadmap and performance measurement matrix. More than enough financial tools, formulae and jargon exist and varying tools are used by organisations to report, what they believe are the relevant measurements for their business' performance. However, each such tool serves a specific objective and thus needs to be viewed accordingly. Ideally, CEOs would not view any individual tool or matrix in isolation without making an effort to understand the ramifications thereof on the wider operations.

Typically, organisations and investors look at performance measurement tools such as book value, Earnings before Interest, Taxes, Depreciation and Amortisation (EBITDA), Earnings Before Interest and Taxes (EBIT), Earnings Per Share (EPS), Price-Earnings ratio (PE) and market capitalisation as barometers to evaluate health of an organisation. However, each of these has its inherent limitations and serves only a specific objective. Book value per share reflects the past, EBITDA and EBIT are used more by lenders to evaluate headroom in cash flows for debt service and market capitalisation is often influenced by speculative positions and forward-looking views taken by the market based upon anticipated future earnings.

A CEO's performance is best evaluated by measurement of EBIT (Earnings before Interest and Tax) and the ratio of EBIT as a percentage of sales, asset deployed, capital employed, and so on.

CEOs need to be held accountable for return on investment or ROI on capital committed under their charge. Smart CEOs will thus be able to strike a good balance between operating efficiency, growth in market share, R&D, and ongoing investments behind assets and the brands. It is important to understand that the long-term is nothing but an aggregate of multiple short terms! Thus, there cannot be a disconnect between the two. More importantly, for an engaged board to evaluate a CEOs performance, the long-term itself must be a quantified duration. Accordingly, the outcome horizon for decisions taken ideally must not spill over the tenure of the incumbent CEOs such that accountability is in place.

The key to sustainable organisational success lies in the CEO recognising that the end game is for him to deliver healthy free cash flows that show an ongoing improvement as a return on sales, assets and capital employed. Other matrices like growth in market share, customer base, expansion into new segments and markets are tools to get there and book value, EPS and market capitalisation is the outcome of the performance.

People

Organisations succeed because they are blessed with wonderful people working for them, generation after generation. Smart CEOs understand that and recognise that the best of production facilities, brands, and distribution systems and so on are of no use if the leadership cannot motivate, groom and keep its workforce fully engaged. People need to feel wanted and they need to believe that irrespective of where they stand in the organisational hierarchy, their individual effort is contributing towards making that difference, and it is worth something. A paycheque cannot buy spirit, commitment, loyalty, dedication and passion for the organisation. It grows within an organisation, with time and it is dependent upon how successive leadership has treated the rank and file of the organisation, its work culture, employee engagement and recognition and reward policies.

During the time Tata Global Beverages owned and ran the largest integrated tea plantations across four states in India, it was blessed with fourth generation labour domiciled on its estates, fully engaged, which had with time become a captive source of filling in vacancies without a problem. More importantly, the company could at will access skilled temporary labour during peak cultivation season, with minimal difficulty. This was a significant competitive advantage for Tata Global Beverages.

The events of 26/11 were harrowing for the country, Mumbai and the Taj. For 72 torturous hours, the Taj Mahal hotel in Mumbai was under siege as were some other locations across the city. However, during that time, not one single employee of the Taj Mahal hotel, who happened to be on duty that fateful evening, left the hotel on his or her own accord. The hotel used to have a half-dozen entry/exits operating around the building and every single employee would have had the opportunity to head for the nearest exit point when considered safe enough to do so. However, not one employee left his or her position and did everything within their power to safeguard the guests and colleagues.

The unique display of courage and the spirit of service before self as was displayed by the Taj Mahal, Mumbai employees is now globally known and recognised. The Taj Mahal had raised the bar yet again for 'guest service' and all this is now documented in a case study at the Harvard Business School. Professor Deshpande who wrote the referred paper refers to the Taj Mahal's employees' behaviour as 'leadership at the bottom!' CEOs that inherit such a workforce are blessed and need to nurse the culture of such passion and dedication amongst the workforce.

The employee engagement program needs to be personally driven by CEOs and it is not enough to just dedicate it to Human Resources. It is the CEO's responsibility to ensure that the organisation's talent retention, attraction, reward, career planning and related people's practices are transparent, true to word, and action demonstrates word. The CEO needs to be seen as being consistently fair and accessible and not allowing a culture of some being 'more equal than the others!'

Among the many CEOs that I worked for, Krishna Kumar was by far, the most humane 'people's CEO' that I came across in my career. In or around 1996, Krishna Kumar, who was the Managing Director of Tata Global Beverages at that time invited Ratan Tata and Noshir Soonawala to visit the company plantations in Munnar. Krishna Kumar had by then been at the helm of affairs in the company for over six years and much had been done already in the district such as the introduction of modern agricultural practices, modernisation of factories, R&D, labour welfare, Corporate Social Responsibility, and so on. It was a good time to showcase Munnar and its achievements to the Group Chairman and Vice Chairman to give them comfort that the shareholder's funds were being wisely deployed. More importantly, the visit would be a huge boost to workforce morale.

The company had a director's bungalow at Munnar named Ladbroke House, built in 1917 by James Finlay, the former Scottish owners, on a four-acre site. By tradition, invitations for a visit to Ladbroke House were rare and few in between for local resident executives. VIP guests visiting Munnar would be accommodated in Ladbroke House only with a prior clearance by the Managing Director and after that all local arrangements were overseen by the General Manager. As per tradition, once in a while, the division's General Manager would invite his Heads of Departments along with spouses for a cocktail party to meet visiting VIPs, and that was it. Thus, there would be scores of executives who would have spent a career in Munnar but never had the occasion to be invited into the haloed Ladbroke House.

During Ratan Tata's visit to Munnar that weekend in 1996, Krishna Kumar chose to break away from past tradition and decided to invite the entire management staff team, along with spouses, for cocktails on the lawns of Ladbroke House to meet Ratan Tata and Noshir Soonawala.

I have a very vivid recollection of that evening and all the arrangements that preceded it. Krishna Kumar and Ratna, his very charming wife, played the ever gracious hosts and introduced Ratan Tata and Noshir Soonawala to the invitees, as they sauntered in making their way past the VIPs. We were half an hour into the evening and Noshir noticed that Krishna Kumar had little difficulty in recalling the names of the couples as they trooped by. Bemused, Noshir commented, "Krishna, I wonder for how long you will remember the names of each couple, as we meet them?" Krishna Kumar just smiled and continued with the introductions, recalling all first names and the functional background of the executives along with the odd anecdote about some.

For a CEO to know not only the management executives of his organisation by the first name but to also know many of the respective spouses by their first names is one of the main qualities that makes him a 'people's CEO. This was just one of the many illustrations of Krishna Kumar's leadership style and the efforts he made to really connect with the employees across the rank and file of the organisation.

Customers

It's important for CEOs to stay connected with their customers and understand their demographics. They need to invest time to delve into where the business is coming from and where the margins are being made. The key to running a successful business lies in a CEO's ability to guide the sales team on which business to chase and which business can be ignored because it is not margin accretive or the turnover from the business will trigger hidden losses. Organisational success thus lies in its ability to not just blindly follow the pack but to always be smart and to allow competition to do dumb things!

It is helpful to get into the psyche of their customers and be able to differentiate what excites the customer and conversely what features of the products or services a customer is indifferent about, but nevertheless is costing the company money to keep delivering. It is in this regard that CEOs must personally review product and service specifications and sign off on the same, weeding out frills that do not add value in the brand promise, or those that the customer is not willing to pay for.

It is often the case that subconsciously organisations incur expenses, merely because they did so in the past. Revenue expenditure too needs the same discipline as one would expect for capital allocation and a zero-based budgeting approach is a good way to begin. Stretching the rupee and good cost management is not about 'stopping and denial' but about enabling an organisation to be in control and to invest smartly towards meeting its customers' expectations and delighting them consistently.

Further, CEOs need to invest time to understand the dynamics of the market, competitor activity and must be in a position to pre-empt trends and emerging needs. As entry barriers progressively weaken, organisations need to keep reinventing their product offerings to retain and strengthen their competitive advantage. Long-term success would be dependent upon an organisation's ability to continuously re-engineer its offerings through better source materials, packaging, product innovation and cost elimination leading to the enhanced customer experience.

The importance of an organisational leadership to understand where the money is being made and which products and markets are at that moment the organisation's cash cows cannot be overstated. These products and markets need to be nursed and investments must be continuously made to protect the core business. The next key lies in the CEO's ability and desire to zero down on those businesses, segments, customers that are not yielding the desired margins and ROI. These need to be focus areas for a time-bound turnaround. The functional leadership needs to be held accountable to deliver this in a measured manner with a clear definition of roles and responsibility.

Finally, perennially loss-making businesses must be weaned out. Time is of the essence and no organisation can afford to carry within it a bouquet of loss leaders that it just does not have the ability or wherewithal to turn around and become profitable.

Customer retention and top-line growth are important but CEOs need to understand that all customer segments and markets do not generate the same yield nor profitability. Thus yield variance needs to be monitored and CEOs need to take the call on those businesses that just cannot be made profitable. I have great admiration for the pioneering work the promotors of Flipkart have done over the years, guiding this company to be India's largest e-commerce company in quick time. Single-handedly taking on the might of Amazon, with the latter's deep pockets, is no mean accomplishment. Having said that, what does bother me a lot is Flipkart's inability to generate profits despite its current scale of operations and over a decade in business. (As per the Standalone Financial Statements of Flipkart India Private Ltd as filed with the Registrar of Companies for the year ending March 31,2017, the company reported a Total Income of Rs. 15,570 crores, an EBITDA loss of Rs. 178 crores and a Loss before Tax of Rs. 244 crores.)

So what went wrong here was, in my view, the incorrect belief that chasing top-line growth at any cost is good for the business on the premise that eventually the captive customers will start contributing to margin improvement. The truth is that it's not a smart strategy to fight for market share leadership of loss-making segments or get into an endless and never ending price war. Flipkart needs to think through an alternate combat plan and create its own unique differentiator positioning! It need not strive to be everything to everybody but create its own niche in a market that is large enough in any case. If a company is not profitable after a decade of operations, its strategy requires a comprehensive relook. The game is no longer about a blind chase of a top-line market share but about growth with sustainable profitability and a return on investments. As path-breaking and pioneering organisations such as Flipkart and MakeMyTrip are, they need to now change their game and realise that long-term survival will not be driven only by a blind chase of top-line growth, at any cost. Eventually, it is all about profitable growth! The pricing that we often see in online retail is potentially a race to the bottom if a course correction is not pursued soon enough. Within the Indian market, the ongoing price wars within the telecom, aviation as also the hospitality sector has done no long-term good for any of the players in the respective sectors.

We need to recognise that once you spoil a customer, the latter remains spoilt and there is little headroom for course correction. CEOs must thus nudge the organisation towards a disciplined and fair relationship with the customer, which needs to be win-win for both.

Leadership must play a very important role in guiding the sales and marketing strategy of the organisation with the clear recognition that their own perceived beliefs and behaviour would influence the behavioural pattern across the organisation and decisions taken across the spectrum would either create value or destroy value. If CEOs lead the charge from the front, the insecurity to deliver top-line growth at any cost gets arrested and any potential value erosion is arrested.

Insecurity makes a lot of people continuously look over their shoulders and blindly follow the pack. But such people are also looking for a leader to break away from the pack and to lead a course correction! In short, a hallmark of great CEOs would be those who not only leave their indelible mark within the organisation, but those who also do so across the industry.

And as I play the game of life
I try to make it better each and every day
And when I struggle in the night
The magic of the music seems to light the way
Intuition takes me there
Intuition takes me everywhere

– John Lennon –

Song: Intuition. **Album:** Working Class Hero. **Record label:** Apple Records.

The Situation Room

Unplugged

In the early eighties, life for accountants was very different from what it is now. That is stating the obvious though!

Audited results were required to be published only once a year, consolidation of subsidiaries and associate companies into the parent company was not required, we still had not discovered the joys of technology and book-keeping was undertaken manually, tallying the Trial Balance was a matter of celebration in the Accounts Department, all offices had a Comptist *(derived from Comptometer, a key driven mechanical calculator)* whose only full-time job was to total manually prepared spreadsheets, day in and day out. We used manual typewriters, white ink for corrections, and telex machines for external communication and cyclostyled reports for circulation.

The stock markets had not evolved, analyst fraternity did not exist, the financial markets were still in an embryonic stage and corporates were borrowing money from banks at 21 percent per annum under the Cash Credit scheme. Corporates had very limited access to foreign currency and were issued an annual foreign currency withdrawal permit by the Reserve Bank of India, on which every transaction relating to foreign currency expenditure was recorded along with the monitoring of the residual unutilised limit, transaction-wise and rubber stamped. The Reserve Bank's prior permission was required even to draw a daily foreign currency allowance for overseas business trips.

The CFO role in those days was focussed on accounting and audits, compliances, fund-raising, capital allocation and the like. Businesses normally grew organically and M&A activities were not common. Nonequity financing options were limited to bank term loans, debentures, intercorporate borrowings and the like.

With time, economic liberalisation within the country unfurled, geographical barriers gradually opened up, capital markets evolved as did the stock markets and most importantly, consumer purchasing power came into being. With all of that and more, corporates started growing their businesses in geometric progression, in India as also overseas and in the changing scenario, the organisational needs, compulsions and mandatory compliance significantly increased. Reflecting back on my own career, during the sixteen-odd years that I was a CFO, my role and focus areas as they were originally in 2000 kept changing and evolving to what they were by the time I hung up my boots in 2016.

Clearly, a CFO's role and thrust areas will vary, across sectors and will also be influenced by the organisation's own individual priorities, issues and agenda. I think that the larger issue here is that in the emerging regulatory and legal environment, besides being a high-pressure job, the CFO's position in listed companies is increasingly becoming a high-risk job as well. Once a CFO puts his signature on a cheque or a Balance Sheet, he is accountable for all the financial decisions taken across the organisation, across multiple offices and geographies, and thus the incumbent becomes continuously accountable for decisions taken by other functional heads, while the vice versa is rarely the case. I make this point as in the course of my career, I did come across a CEO who had the great wisdom to issue a companywide circular stating to the effect that under his new administration, Financial Controllers across all business units would henceforth report only to the business head and would have no reporting relationship, dotted or otherwise, into the CFO, unless a scam took place. Hallelujah!

I do believe that the effectiveness of a CFO is substantially dependent on his equation with the CEO and the latter's willingness to let the CFO have a free hand in getting the job done.

In present times, I would reckon that almost all CFOs would be devoting a considerable amount of time on six key business aspects, among others, which would include business strategy, capital raising and allocation, service and support to operations, dealing with the investor community, board affairs and finally, technology.

Business Strategy

Over the years, CFOs have played a significant role in facilitating the formulation of the organisation's business strategy. In a manner of speaking, the finance function is like a glue that binds an organisation together, connects all the dots, is one function that interfaces with all other business verticals, in some form or the other, and thus places the CFO in a unique position to gather and place insights and perspectives in front of the CEO that otherwise may not necessarily be visible.

With their intimate knowledge of the organisation, a CFO knows where the money is being made and where the margins are lacking, what can be undertaken more cost-effectively and have a view on what need not be done at all. More importantly, CFOs need to keep an eye on the future all the time, and facilitate decision-making based upon the probable financial impact on the organisation of the multiple initiatives already underway within the organisation.

Monitoring External Influences

My view is that the days of putting together a medium-term four to five years strategic plan in place, running it past the board, seeking their buy-in and thereafter, getting into an execution mode 'eyes wide shut' is now all passé. In the present scenario, a good business strategy calls for managing change and the disruption being caused in the market due to the multiple extraneous factors, some visible and others that need to be pre-empted. The various uncertainties around global markets call for a much sharper focus and measurement of the near-term external variables that will have a game-changing impact on the long-term health and sustainability of the organisation.

Organisations are very often caught up in all the pressures of the day-to-day running of the business, meeting the monthly volume and sales targets, and so on due to which we at times take our eye off the ball and do not see the strong undercurrents forcing the need for change in the way business is being run.

Thus, we are often not ready to pre-empt what is threatening to take place and anticipate consequences thereof on the organisation, either as an opportunity that needs to be addressed or a new risk that needs a mitigation plan. The biggest mistake that an organisation can make is to persist with what it has succeeded in doing in the past, in the blind belief that it will work well in the future too. Little do we realise that the future will hit us like a runaway freight train if the organisation gets complacent. It's evident that in today's times, competition, markets and consumers can be brutal when it comes to an overnight switch away from a brand merely because other options are in play.

It is necessary, thus for CFOs to ensure that more than adequate care has been taken to scan the environment, look into the future and quantify new emerging risks and threats that could snowball into a problem for the sector, and thus for an organisation.

The Emergence of Non-Traditional Competition

For the hospitality sector, the emergence and growth of Airbnb has been a revelation and a development that has changed the rules of the game permanently. The hospitality segment has traditionally grown around the world, anchored by well-established branded hotel chains. Such hotel chains expanded their businesses, globally, not just by leveraging their own Balance Sheets, but also by getting into partnership with asset owners who were willing to invest in hotel real estate, to be managed by the hotel chains on behalf of the former.

Generally, the unbranded free-standing hotels struggled to earn a premium on their room tariffs on account of their inability to reach out to a larger customer base in source markets and their inconsistent product and service delivery. So, besides the need to be able to access capital required to fund greenfield growth, a robust distribution system was a prerequisite to survive and flourish in the market.

Airbnb has overnight changed all of that and closer home, OYO has made significant inroads as well. Further disruption in the market has been triggered by the MakeMyTrips of the world. What such online aggregators and booking engines have done is in quick time expand the supply of rooms, across markets, at a pace that is unprecedented, simply by connecting free-standing unbranded inventory to the customer, which hitherto were not visible. The amazing accomplishment is that these companies now control a huge inventory of rooms, across markets and price points, without owning any hotel assets whatsoever. Around the world now, private residences, inns, guest houses, holiday homes, villas, apartments, and so on are available for the well-heeled traveller, to be hired out at the push of a button. For the moment this space is catering substantially to the leisure segment, but with time, the disruption will grow and individual business travellers will also explore these wider options. This is a serious wake-up call for the organised branded hotel chains across the industry.

Regulatory Changes

Strategy formulation must take into account the emerging regulatory changes that are sweeping across all economies, the impact of some of which can have adverse implications for the business. Under the recent change in government in the United States, the restrictions being imposed on immigrant labour wishing to come into the United States, and many who are already working within the United States on a valid work permit is a case in point. While the media has limited its coverage highlighting the potential impact of such changed regulations on the IT sector, the reality is that this will impact all corporates who have invested in the United States and operate businesses in that market. CFOs have to devote increased resources and time to continuously scan the environment, across markets, to identify such emerging external risks across markets and help the CEO put in place a risk mitigation strategy.

Risk of Currency Rate Oscillation

Strategy execution calls for capital deployment, and capital does not come cheap. Even great business decisions, well thought through take time to execute, have long gestation periods, and thus the intervening period between blueprint and roll out needs to be managed. The CFO must make sure that capital locked in underperforming or non-core assets is monetised, such that the earnings dilution risks are minimised and cost-effective liquidity is in place to fund growth behind priority areas.

In recent times, the volatility of currencies and interest rates has changed the rules of the game permanently. In fact, the volatility is so severe, which coupled with speculative forces, renders any scientific forecasting of an organisation's exposure to multi-currency risk rather difficult.

During my time with Indian Hotels, between 2005 and 2010, as a part of its expansion and global drive, the company acquired assets in the United States, South Africa, Australia, Thailand, and so on. Each such acquisition was funded partly by equity from the parent company and the balance through appropriate debt, raised in foreign currency and housed in the asset-owning SPV or special-purpose vehicle.

In a couple of years with the weakening of the INR, and many other currencies against the US dollar, the viability of the investments, the outstanding debt and the financial performance of the underlying assets was very different to what the company had originally visualised it to be. In particular, the weakening of the INR against the basket of currencies that Indian Hotels was exposed to had an adverse impact on the company's profitability. Across the company's several overseas subsidiaries, local currencies too weakened against the US dollar, thereby causing significant foreign currency losses that were not foreseen. These were new unexpected risks that the company had to manage as the currency oscillation impacted the operating profits, return on investments and separately bloated the value of foreign currency debt on local Balance Sheets. This was, unfortunately, the case across corporate India.

Just the pressure to service a US dollar denominated debt, from earnings in local currency, wipes away the visibility of any improvement in operating performance of the underlying overseas assets. The volatility of cross-currency rate movements is essentially a new risk that now needs to be managed.

The point here is that it's now incumbent upon the CFOs to walk the CEOs and the leadership team through the emerging new reality, which is that the battle for leadership and profits is not just about the product, customers and markets. All of this is now substantially influenced by global factors over which we have no control and limited visibility. Such changes can render many business assumptions infructuous, within a short span of time. Thus, strategy formulation will need to be underpinned by a comprehensive scan of the environment, going well beyond traditional business-related parameters, the impact of which will influence which way the organisation needs to go and why.

Fund-Raising and Capital Allocation

Long-term fund-raising for a business is a fine art. For long-term financing, clearly, equity financing is the most expensive way to fund growth, as the return on equity that an organisation needs to service is invariably higher than the cost of debt. Plus, equity once infused into an organisation needs to be serviced in perpetuity, barring the rare instances of capital reduction in the future, through rare equity buyback schemes.

Equity Call

New equity infusion is a call that the board would take bearing in mind the principal shareholder's desire not to be diluted, the proposed pricing for the intended equity issue and the attractiveness of the discount over prevalent market price, the dilution impact post equity issue on market capitalisation, and so on. The pricing sensitivity cannot be overstated, as from the perspective of existing shareholders, the lower the issue price to market, the better it is for shareholders. Conversely, from the organisation's perspective, the discount over market price needs to be well balanced to ensure that the overall expansion in the equity base is serviceable by the organisation in the future and the dividend payout ratio is maintained on the expanded equity base.

Traditional Rights issue of equity in India is a very cumbersome affair for raising funds. The entire process calls for the preparation of a very comprehensive Information Memorandum about the company and the objectives of the fund-raising for the Security and Exchange Board of India's for scrutiny and prior approval. This calls for arrangers, bankers, lawyers and underwriters to the proposed issue to be brought into play to advise on regulatory compliances and disclosures, etc. In effect, the entire process can take over six months to complete, at the risk of the markets turning adversely during the intervening period and impacting the intended outcome of the fund-raising.

Alternate options to raise equity include preferential allotment of equity to promoters, linked to market price, which thus entails the least capital expansion. A qualified institutional placement or QIP issue would, however, dilute all existing shareholders. Other avenues for raising capital would include a possible equity issue to the public with differential voting rights, preference shares issue, and so on.

Besides raising financing through equity issue, the residual medium to long-term needs are addressed through leveraging the Balance Sheet and raising debt financing. Typically, debt raised would be secured and would be serviced through the future cash flows of the organisation and would be progressively retired on the strength of the future cash flows of assets being created. But that is only the theory.

It is rather obvious to state that CFOs need to play a critical role in helping shape up a healthy balance in the debt/equity mix of an organisation's capital employed at any point in time. Debt is good, if managed well and deployed intelligently, as besides providing a tax break on interest cost, it helps shore up ROI.

An ongoing dialogue with the credit rating agencies is necessary to ensure that they are well versed with the sector and the organisational strategic intent, as any drop in rating impacts the cost of raising new debt.

The fact of the matter is that there are too many factors that come into play, that influence the emerging debt-equity play of a company. Balance Sheets could change their quality and character at short notice if new assets acquired underperform beyond acceptable tolerance in terms of time horizon and economic returns. Like a river in spate breaking its bank, a stressed Balance Sheet too can force an unprepared organisation to change course!

Many years ago, Indian Hotels had made an open offer to acquire 100% of the outstanding Class A listed shares of Belmond Hotels Ltd (formerly known as Orient-Express Hotels Ltd), a company registered in Bermuda and listed on the New York Stock Exchange. Before making the bid, Indian Hotels had acquired from the open market around 12 percent of the target company shares.

As is now probably well known to the reader, the Board of Belmond Hotels spurned Indian Hotel's overtures and after that, undertook a series of privately placed equity issues to raise new capital resulting in Indian Hotel's stake in the former declining to a low 7 percent on account of the resultant dilution! While this was permitted under American law, it would not have been possible under Indian regulations without prior shareholders' approval. So here is an illustration of a board that goes and dilutes all its existing shareholders, without blinking, and it was fine!

Back home in India, the Leela Group is gasping and many of its hotel assets have been placed on the block by the asset reconstruction company or the ARC, as the promoters did not have the foresight to raise equity when the market capitalisation of the company was attractive. Even at the cost of dilution, the promoters could still have stayed in control of the company, managed its fund flows more elegantly and not have had to face the risk of the business going bankrupt on account of leverage beyond any acceptable tolerance. It is not at all unhelpful to lean back on classic textbook financial management tools and guidance when it comes to managing Balance Sheet health.

Capital Deployment

The boards need to play a very proactive role in capital deployment, facilitated by diagnostics presented by the CFO of the management's business case. Allocation of resources must ensure a fine balance between investing behind the good health of existing assets and operations as also investing to expand and grow the business for the future. Too much focus on the latter, at the cost of the former, can be detrimental to the organisation.

Return on Investment

The importance of measurement and monitoring of the payback and ROI of new investments, in other words, assumptions as were tabled in the business plans, cannot be overstated. Organisations do not often devote the required time and effort to monitor the post-investment performance of new assets. The boards need to step in and ensure that this becomes a point for review, as a process, in board meetings.

The CEO and the management team need to be held accountable for the post-investment performance of assets. In this regard, the boards must be able to sift through and segregate a review of post-investment ROI as against operating cash flows that need to be generated by the assets, which are unrelated to the value of the original investment itself. By implication, post-acquisition performance review of new businesses must not get clouded by subsequent opinions on 'did we pay/invest right?' The point really is that that the CEO and the management team are obliged to deliver the operating margins from newly acquired assets, which is unrelated to the cost at which such assets were acquired. Boards must be smart not to allow management to confuse and mix the two issues.

In today's time, CFOs need to spend considerable time to study the capital markets; they must be aware of market sentiments and trends, interest rate movements and the ongoing impact of currency rates on business.

The Art of Balance Sheet Management

The efficiency with which CFOs manage their Balance Sheets, pre-empt the ongoing capital needs of the organisation and thus have a game plan in place, with well thought out options and timelines, is a key to ensuring the long-term health of the organisation. This needs to be anchored by the ability to pre-empt and facilitate course correction, well before a situation gets out of hand.

Between 2005 and 2009, the hospitality sector in India and around the world went through a bull run. Indian Hotels by themselves had a great run too and reported record profits and strong cash flows. Accordingly, as a part of the company's growth agenda, substantially, all of the cash retention was ploughed back by the company to expand capacity across markets in India and selectively overseas as well, in key feeder markets.

With the Indian economy booming and expected to continue to grow rapidly, most international chains had made a belated inroad into the domestic market, and thus, it was important for Indian Hotels to grow rapidly too within the domestic market in order to protect its share of hotel room supply, which is a precursor to protecting and enhancing the market share of customers.

Thus, at a time when the company's annual consolidated EBITDA was near about Rs. 1000 crores, and expected to grow further, a four times EBITDA leverage was felt to be sustainable and acceptable as per industry standards. During this time, the company acquired assets in New York, Boston, Sydney, Cape Town, San Francisco along with the purchase of the Class A shares in Belmond Hotels Ltd. In India too, the company grew across markets, leveraging the Balance Sheets of the parent company and some of the JVs and associate companies within the Taj Group.

However, by the time this particular investment cycle was over, the company was hit by the fallout of the global financial meltdown, the ripple effect of which impacted the Indian economy as well. So not only did the overseas markets the company had invested in slow down, but the key Indian domestic market itself tanked, the pain of which was accentuated by the new hotel room capacity that had already been added by various industry players. It was a 'perfect storm' that the company had walked into. To add to its woes, the debt level, which the company was originally comfortable with suddenly looked very discomforting. Something needed to be done, and really fast.

After a careful assessment of the situation and realistic reading of the market, it was clear that it would not be easy to get the profitability and cash flows back to where the company needed them to be quickly. The markets had been scorched and it was going to be a long and slow painful haul back to the top.

Thus, a combination of financial and debt restructuring initiatives were thought through and put in place. These included refinancing some of the INR debt with long-term tenure to ease any near-term principle repayment pressures, raising debentures with a low coupon coupled with a rear-loaded premium on redemption, shifting offshore subsidiary debt on to the parent company to avail a tax break locally. The company felt that it was pointless to house debt in any offshore subsidiary if it was not capable of servicing it independently from its own operating cash flows. In addition, the company also undertook selective interest rate swaps, migrating to US$ LIBOR, thereby further reducing the impact of interest costs on the Profit and Loss account. With a combination of the aforementioned initiatives, the company was able to cap the cost of interest on the Indian Hotel's standalone Profit and Loss account to well inside of 5 percent per annum, thereby enabling it to tide over a very difficult time.

While the preceding was a big relief, it was clearly not enough as the company needed to find the cash to retire a fair amount of debt, and in quick time, as some of the acquisitions were not going to deliver cash flows anywhere close to the original expectations. The markets had just changed too dramatically throwing many past business assumptions by the wayside.

So, the next wave of reforms was to identify underperforming or non-core assets for divestment to generate the liquidity to whittle down the debt and thereby create the liquidity to invest behind new priorities. In this phase, the company divested its ownership of the hotels in Sydney and Boston along with finally divesting its entire stake in Belmond Hotels Ltd, amongst others. In the case of the Boston hotel, the company negotiated a back to back management services agreement with the buyer to retain brand presence within the market, while monetising the asset. The asset divestment proceeds were utilised by the company entirely to retire debt.

The last initiative, and probably the most complicated and time-consuming was the restructuring of the holding of all the company's overseas investments. For legacy reasons, these were scattered across subsidiaries and JVs, across multiple jurisdictions. These were all shifted into IHOCO NV, a single offshore fully owned subsidiary of Indian Hotels, as the management believed that the 'whole' once housed together within a single legal entity would be much more valuable than the 'sum of the parts' of such investments.

In a manner of speaking, while the management continued to be focused on improving the operating cash flows from the business, the Balance Sheet restructuring that the company undertook concurrently saved the day for it.

As the business expands and the enterprise enters unchartered overseas markets, there are new hidden risks that we progressively get exposed to. This risk is the impact of the movement of multiple currencies, against each other, and on the parent company's profitability and Balance Sheet. Currency movements are influenced by far too many geopolitical factors and investment decisions and capital calls must take these into account.

Here too, boards now need to devote more time to understanding the dynamics of 'what if' scenarios on the operations and business on account of adverse currency movements. It's important for boards to spend time on understanding the impact of a multi-currency play on the profitability of organisations while reviewing offshore investment proposals. The importance of this cannot be overstated.

As the Executive Director and CFO of Indian Hotels, one of my biggest challenge, perpetually, was how to ensure that the various operating and asset-owning companies within the Taj Group of Hotels were adequately funded, day in and day out, and business was not impacted for want of capital. The challenge here really was that 70 percent or more of the Taj Group's assets were housed across joint ventures, associate companies, subsidiaries or were assets under management contracts. In such a scenario, the overall brand portfolio was sitting upon a complex legal structure of ownership that the end customer was ignorant of or indifferent to. The perpetual challenge was how to ensure a seamless guest experience across the portfolio in the event of an asset owner's reluctance or inability to plough back the required capital into the business, thereby jarring guest experience.

This is increasingly becoming a perennial problem in the hospitality sector where asset owners are taking advantage of the 'operators' and the latter's insecurity of not wanting to lose market presence. Often, insecurity displayed by the operator and thus a reluctance not to call the bluff of an errant asset owner is exploited by the latter, with operators being compelled to infuse capital shortfall into the business, and subordinating their fee, and other such measures in favour of asset owners. This increasing trend will have a detrimental impact on the brand pull of hotel chains.

Operations

I do believe that it is important and very helpful for the incumbent CFOs to have worked in and been exposed to the front line of operations covering production, sales and marketing, projects, and other functions to really understand business from a non-financial perspective as well. CFOs often need to ask 'why' and often need to say 'no,' which at times leads to an organisation force fitting a CFO into the image of a person who is 'not facilitating' but is 'an obstruction.' In reality, because of the complexities that the CFO is dealing with, such as allocating limited capital among multiple demands, intimate knowledge of the front-end of the business goes a long way in adding credibility to questions that a CFO raises during the review and his ability to thereby present a balanced perspective to a contrarian view.

Frontline Orientation

In the course of my career, I had the good fortune of being rotated into financial assignments across the businesses that I worked for, covering sales, marketing, commodity trading, exports and production, and related functions. Such an exposure acquired during my middle management days helped me gain insights into the business, which otherwise I probably would not have been exposed to if I had continued to look at financial decision-making while sitting in a corporate office.

Knowledge of the nuts and bolts of the business thus helps in getting behind the numbers into the underlying activity itself, such as investments being asked for, the fine print of how intended funds will be deployed and greater clarity about the end game. More importantly, such an exposure helps finance executives look at the business through the lens of operations and sales, people on the frontline, and thereby being in the position to empathise with the day-to-day pressures of meeting production and sales targets.

It is indeed desirable for CFOs to ensure that the finance team is well-trained to capture accurate data consistently, that the data interpretation is correct, and diagnostics undertaken are logical and backed up by facts and rationale.

I have always believed that at any point in time, two questions can be raised. The first is 'do we really need to do this at all' and the second is 'can we do this differently?' The other question that I always raised in my mind, before I formed a view was 'does the customer see value in this?' There is so much that we do in a business, spend money on an activity because 'we did so in the past' that we fail to take a pause and ask the question 'are we making a difference that the customer sees as *value* and thus it's a good investment, or are we doing so merely because of competition?'

FMCG companies that run seasonal promotions to push sales often give away a variety of freebies. While this is a long-standing industry practice, one needs to ask the question whether the consumer saw value in that giveaway product or has the consumer discarded the giveaway, not seeing any value therein, while the organisation continues to incur costs in the belief that it's good for business.

Giveaways are a huge problem in the hospitality business with very significant hidden cost. The industry is blindly perpetuating past practices of throwing in free airport pickups, bottled water, wine bottles, fruits, unlimited free Wi-Fi, happy hours in the bars, and so on, all of which costs a lot, erode margins and in an environment of declining tariffs, are practices that the industry needs to wean away from. The solution lies in focussing on a consistent product and service experience for the guest and if that is the case, the guest will be indifferent to the freebies. Consistent delivery of a guest experience in line with the brand promise, in any case, enhances the brand pull.

CFOs need to work with the CEO and the CXOs to help change the mindset. This way the finance team can participate in influencing 'what will happen' as against mechanically reporting 'what did happen!'

Resource Deployment

Financial controls, discipline, and so on is not just about questioning the need to spend. CFOs also need to ensure that the right kind of capital is being redeployed back within the organisation, which is necessary to ensure the long-term health of the business. Questions need to be asked if the right investments have been made and factored into the business plan for Repairs and Maintenance and replacement of the assets and that short-term pressures are not influencing decisions that can impact the long-term health and business sustainability. Similarly, consumer-facing businesses need to keep investing in new products and the brands to keep them vibrant and fresh, which is necessary to enhance brand recall and salience.

In my experience, working capital management, monthly cash flow review, the age of receivables and idle non-moving inventory, etc. are hidden costs and inefficiencies that we allow to creep into a business. Organisations make the mistake of allowing CXOs to take business decisions that relax pre-agreed norms and leave the subsequent remedial action in the hands of the accountants. There is no point in closing the barn doors after the horses have bolted!

The hidden cost of company money circulating in the market as uncollected sales proceeds unsecured and thus at risk is a matter that needs tight monitoring and review. The organisation needs to recognise that a sale is not closed unless the sale proceeds have been realised. It is actually quite simple. The organisation's credit norms, presumably benchmarked with industry practice, need to be sacrosanct and deviations need to be controlled.

Inventory management itself is an art and efficient Purchase Managers working in tandem with operations and finance can keep things in order by vendor, product and SKU (stock keeping unit) rationalisation. Non-moving and slow-moving inventory must be periodically cleaned up. Finance managers need a good understanding of the raw material and consumables, delivery lead time, consumption pattern and based upon that, ideal inventory levels should be worked out. It is not complicated, but we have a tendency to complicate very simple things because we are not interested enough to keep improving.

In the front-end of the business, smart finance executives can monitor indents placed with production and despatches with the floating stocks at the Carry and Forwarding points to ensure that the trade is not being overloaded with stock supplies, at quarter end, just to meet sale volume targets. Needless to say, such dumping of stock with the trade leads to the risk of sale recall, ageing of goods while in storage and collection defaults.

The reason that I have raised such fundamental and basic issues is that, in my belief, an organisation needs to keep raising the bar on operating efficiencies and cost rationalisation to remain combative in the marketplace.

Turf wars are underway, across sectors, and many businesses are fighting bitter battles for a top-line share in the belief that once you have a share of the wallet, the share of the margins will be a natural corollary. Nothing can be further from the truth. If we do not manage our costs, there will be no correlation between top-line growth and the emerging bottom-line. Costs have to be controlled and an organisation must continuously question past practices that can be discontinued as they are no longer of any relevance. That is often the case.

Organisations often tend to become a victim of the 'rhinoceros syndrome' which means just charging down in one direction, eyes wide shut, without a pause to look around and re-evaluate. It's best to be prepared rather than trying to assemble a parachute after having jumped off a cliff.

Investors and Analysts

Dealing with the investors and analysts community is now taking up a considerable amount of time for the CFOs, and for all the right reasons.

Listening to Shareholders

Functioning as a bridge between the promotor shareholders and the board as also other significant non-promotor shareholders of the company is a key priority for CFOs. The importance of this cannot be overstated. During my years as CFO, I always recognised and was sensitive to the fact that while I was working for the House of Tatas, who are 40 percent shareholders of the company that I worked for, the residual 60 percent shareholding of the company needed to be kept engaged and their voices had to be heard too. More importantly, the perspective of significant non-promotor shareholders needed to be communicated to the board, through the Investor Affairs Committees, on a regular basis to ensure alignment at all levels.

Way back in 2000, when I took over as the CFO of Tata Global Beverages, I realised that the investor community had as yet not fully comprehended the business model of the company in the domestic market. The company was then the country's largest tea plantation company with a front-end FMCG style branded tea business. The model was complicated because of the huge seasonality that is inherent in plantation production, the tea price commodity cycle and other variables. An understanding of the business became further complicated with the acquisition of The Tetley Group. Investors, analysts, banks, and other such vested interests had many questions and concerns that needed to be addressed and clarified. In fact, we had issues with our credit rating agency too as it refused to believe that the acquisition debt raised by us and housed on The Tetley Group's Balance Sheet was 'non-recourse' to Tata Global Beverages and thus there was no case for the company's standalone debt on its Balance Sheet to come up for a review or a downgrade on account of the consolidated leverage.

In the early days, these were issues of significance that needed to be addressed as consolidation and publication of quarterly financials had not become mandatory as yet. There was thus the need to break up the businesses of Tata Global Beverages in to three logical subsects covering the plantation business, the domestic tea branded business and separately the Tetley business itself, and explain to the analyst community the dynamics of each, where the capital was invested, where the value lay and where the risks and challenges were.

I recall, our credit rating agency was hell-bent on downgrading Tata Global Beverages' rating as the concept of non-recourse debt was rather alien to them and they refused to believe that if for any reason the acquisition faltered, the company had no legal obligation to meet Tetley's debt servicing obligation. The lender's sole remedy was limited to a charge on all of the Tetley assets only, with no recourse to the holding company. Such out of the ordinary business structures required continuous dialogue and articulation across all significant investors and analysts to help them understand the transformation that Tata Global Beverages was undergoing, and how the company was addressing and protecting the interests of its investors and lenders.

Analysts

All through my career, I have observed a rather contradictory sentiment in the market and its response to an organisation's pursuit of aggressive growth. Markets do want companies to grow and expand, else profitability will stagnate and eventually decline. However, markets are also sceptical and risk-averse. This contradiction is understandable as the external environment does not have enough information and data to take a measured view on investment calls that management takes.

The CFO thus has to be clear and forthright about why the proposed investment is good for the business, identify the strategic need, elaborate the benefits, identify the risks and articulate the risk mitigation strategy. More importantly, the post-investment performance of the acquired assets needs to be commented upon to avoid speculation and misinformation in the trade. In particular, the market would want to know the post-investment impact on earnings per share or EPS, and if it is initially dilutive, the timelines within which EPS accretion is expected to be visible, facilitated by the acquired assets.

A formal quarterly interaction with the analysts is now the order of the day when the audited quarterly financial results are published. It is important to unambiguously explain the financial results to the community, clearly isolating any non-recurring gain or loss, such that the quality of operating cash and margins are deciphered correctly by all.

When Rakesh Sarna took over as the Managing Director and CEO of Indian Hotels, once he had settled down and taken stock, I felt I needed to introduce him to the analyst community quickly as it was important for them to get an insight into the man's mind and the direction the new CEO would want the company to move towards. So we did arrange a 'non-agenda' driven interaction with the analysts within the first few months and sure enough, it was a session worth its while.

In the course of the interaction, an analyst asked Rakesh to name three specific measures that the analyst could expect to be company priority under Rakesh's charge. Rakesh's initial response was that the intent was to show quarter to quarter 'progression.' However, the analyst was not satisfied and insisted on specific and measurable criteria to monitor company performance and progress. To that Rakesh subsequently responded by stating that his focus would be on growth, EBITDA margins and EPS improvement. The point here is very simple. Analysts do not like ambiguity.

Communication

The government has also recognised the importance of the ongoing communication between management and the investor/analyst community and has now mandated that management must inform the stock exchange in advance of any scheduled meeting with investors/

analysts, with particulars of attendees. This is a move in the right direction as for the management it is important to ensure that any company related information is uniformly percolated down the system to those who are interested. Thus, putting up the corporate presentation on the website helps.

Dealing with the analysts' community is science as also an art. It's a science insofar as the CFO needs to ensure that all company information and quarterly financials that are published are explained in such an unambiguous manner that all readers draw the same meaning from the same. All of this calls for an elegant articulation of company strategy, sector trends, operating margins after isolating non-recurring events, and the like.

The element of art comes into play in the ability of the CFO being able to sift through the multitude of analysts firms wishing to meet the management and issue reports on the company, to segregate between the credible players and the balance. While interaction with the community is important, what is more relevant is to ensure that firms that have credibility among the foreign institutional investors or the FIIs and domestic investors will cover the company and that their research team has a good grip on the sector and within that the company's business structure based upon data in the public domain.

Disclosures in Shareholder Communication

With recent introduction of a variety of new sections and provisions in the Companies Act 2013 and related governance and compliance protocol as prescribed by SEBI, companies now need to increasingly approach the shareholders for prior approval, through postal ballots, for a variety of business issues, that in the past were not necessarily mandated to require such prior and specific approvals.

While this is a move in the right direction, as it covers even all material subsidiaries, organisations now need to ensure that the communication to the shareholders needs to be very elegantly drafted, unambiguous, and not open to multiple interpretations, and be backed up by a comprehensive explanatory note to each proposed shareholders resolution. This is necessary not just from a governance perspective but in the organisation's interest itself.

Investor Advisory Firms

In recent years, a variety of firms have sprung up that play the role of a vigilante on behalf of shareholders, and keep an eye on all company Annual Reports, quarterly results as also the various resolutions that the management places in front of the shareholders for their approval. Such investor advisory firms, based upon their scrutiny of information provided by management, issue a report to their subscribing members recommending that either member should vote for and support the proposed resolutions, or conversely, the recommendation is to oppose the proposed resolutions. My view is that this rather new process is as yet in its nascent stage and will evolve. It's necessary for such advisory firms to interact with the management and seek suitable clarifications on the subject matter and only after that draw a conclusion. My past experience showed that not necessarily all advisories were issued based upon a well-researched and knowledgeable insight of facts and information already in the public domain.

Investor Advisory reports are now ever increasingly influencing non-promoter shareholder voting pattern and have a big impact on the outcome of shareholder ballots. With a strong presence of the FIIs across listed Indian companies, the former relies upon such reports and often cast their votes aligned to the recommendations of the advisory firms.

In essence, effective communication with the investors and analysts can be enabled by management by ensuring that the community fully understands the company's business model, there is visibility on comparing own performance versus the performance of the competition on similar points, one-off non-recurring transactions are clearly isolated and disclosed in quarterly results, and most importantly the management walks the talk by progressively delivering upon the promise and initiatives spoken about.

One more important constituent that CFOs need to deal with is the media and how they interpret and report on the company performance or any new initiative announced in public. This invariably is a challenge and very often different elements of the media have been found wanting in their understanding of the business, performance and thus on how and what they report. A crisp and concise company release is necessary to ensure that it is interpreted uniformly and reported upon unambiguously.

Technology

Non-technology companies often do not devote adequate time and resources towards innovation the like of which can lead to improved product and services delivery to the end consumer. Not enough is being done in this space and thus the risk of being caught blindsided is high. The key issue here is that with time, entry barriers are progressively dismantling and with shrinking markets and ever-increasing competition, organisations will need to re-engineer and innovate to create the new differentiator that makes them stand apart from the herd, else brands stand the risk of getting commoditised.

Driving the technology strategy of an organisation is often a challenge in a non-technology company. Traditional brick and mortar businesses often do not keep pace with technology innovations that are already underway in the market, which can help an organisation not just retain but also enhance its competitive edge. Conversely, at times companies could end up investing in initiatives that are not necessarily value-accretive to the business. This dilemma can lead an organisation to fall into a clichéd trap all the time trying to 'catch-up' on lost ground, as against taking the lead.

At the outset, I have to confess upfront that I cannot claim to be technology savvy by any stretch of the imagination. However, by virtue of being CFO, I did get an opportunity to play a role in facilitating the rollout of the technology strategy for the two businesses that I worked for. To be effective in this, I chose to rely strongly on my CTO or Chief Technology Officer and spent time with them to understand the architecture of technology as it existed within the organisation, as step one.

The next and more important dialogue was for me to ensure that the CTO fully understood the organisational structure, business needs in the customer-facing activities and back of the house, pain points and thus from all of that, we would strategise on our needs, compulsions and opportunities.

In my mind, I would clearly segregate the compulsion to invest behind 'upgrades' to just run 'as is' processes as against game-changing initiatives.

In 2000, after the acquisition of The Tetley Group by Tata Global Beverages, I was a part of a four-man team, comprising of two each from either side, which worked together to integrate the operations of the two businesses seamlessly. Among other things, the harmonisation of technology-driven business processes was a part of my remit. Tetley was well ahead of Tata Global Beverages so far as technology support was concerned and Tata Global Beverages had some serious catching up to do. Enterprise Resource Planning or ERP was the need of the hour for us, back then, and a rollout of SAP is what we embarked upon. Since by then we had already made up our minds to progressively exit from the plantation business, we chose to roll out the ERP platform across all our business processes, barring green leaf production and related plantation activities. Investments in technology need to be backed up by a clear prior assessment of all new delivery models in the market, their capability and potential and more importantly ensuring that all the organisational needs will be met and addressed by what we propose to acquire. Once the technical evaluation is undertaken, it is equally important to undertake a comprehensive valuation of all the fine print in the vendors proposal, as often when one is negotiating with a vendor covering key business processes, the organisation can unknowingly be at the mercy of the vendor for future 'forced technology upgrades,' or else the ongoing support for the past products will be withdrawn. This has increasingly become an issue with very large global vendors who dominate the technology space! Along with vendor evaluation, it helps to acquire a knowledge partner who facilitates implementation and who can challenge the vendor on our behalf and keep the firm on its toes to ensure that we get what we paid for.

Migration from existing platforms to new emerging technology does cause disruption within the organisation; resistance to change, and mindset does at times come into play. This calls for an upfront communication, strong training that helps adaptation and acceptance of the change as an 'easy to use tool.' If such preparatory work is not undertaken, there is a risk of the investments not being utilised to full potential.

Investments in technology upgrade and migration of business processes from manual to online must be backed up by a clear pre-investment wish list of measurable deliverables for either a cost reduction or a business enhancer and thereby a margin enhancer. Technology must be used to strengthen and build an organisation's competitive edge. Having said that, it's a complicated game as there are far too many products in the market and the trick lies in an organisation's ability to zero down on what works best for them. Invest wisely, and in the right business process and do not make the mistake of over-investing in what will not add value.

In Indian Hotels, some three years ago, the company realised that it needed to take a quantum jump across the board to just 'catch-up' before it could even think of being in a position to claim to be a differentiator. The markets had dramatically changed, the competition was fierce, and aggregators had dramatically changed the way business was flowing through the funnel, with the cost of acquiring businesses climbing up.

After a considerable deliberation, we realised that as against running a fully sourced in-house IT team, perhaps the time had come for the company to outsource its IT administration as there was no way we could internally keep pace with technology changes that were revolutionising not just the sector, but generally the way we ran our lives. With that decision taken, we got TCS on board as our knowledge partners, to hold our hands, and help the Taj design and unfurl its new technology strategy, aligned to the larger organisational business strategy, and get us over the hump.

I guess the trick to success in such an initiative lies in not biting off more than we can chew, being clear of what the priorities are and investing time, money and energy in game-changing initiatives. This calls for clear segregation between 'must have, 'nice to have' and 'not a priority at all.'

Unlike in Tata Global Beverages, where the business processes were rather traditional and had a lot of commonality with other sectors, hospitality is a very different kettle of fish.

For the hospitality sector, in a manner of speaking, the customer engagement cycle ideally needs to touch a potential customer's dream and desire to go on a vacation, converting the dream to intent, the research undertaken by the customer to zero in on the desired option, the subsequent hotel and travel bookings process and experience, the travel and hotel-stay experience itself, and finally, any expression of agony, ecstasy or indifference about the stay experience that might be articulated by the customer across social media or other forums.

Hotel chains can and do influence the dream element in the mind of a potential customer through painstakingly investing in the brands, communication and advertising and thus ensuring that the brand has a 'pull' and is top of the mind in the recall. However, where hotel chains are weak is that they do not have any kind of control or a positive influence on the minds of the customer as he goes through his research, either online or assisted by travel agents, to zero in on probable options.

Traditionally, hotels do have a good grip on speedy facilitating of reservation inquiries and bookings. But that is limited to only those customers who have zeroed in on us, post their research. The ones that got away, the industry would have no knowledge or control over.

The next element of the customer's interaction with the brand is obviously the stay itself, which is the single link in the entire chain over which the hoteliers have full control and can thus ensure 'guest delight' repeatedly. Not that this is always the case, but it is possible.

Finally, we come to a new emerging play in this drama, which is the post-stay feedback, comments, nice things or nasty things a guest might say about his/her experience in social media. Unfortunately, there is precious little that a brand can control after a comment is out in public, barring a defensive explanation.

The point really is for the organisation to figure out where to invest money, to catch the guests' attention, all of which facilitates growth in business and profitability.

In Indian Hotels, as step one, the company had decided to focus on a combination of a must do catch-up, coupled with a desire to invest in enablers and game changers concurrently. The technology upgrade program thus encompassed an across the board upgrade in property management systems, the point of sale, loyalty program, guest recognition, the website, data analytics, social media, and so on.

Once investment decisions are taken, the project management calls for vigilant monitoring to ensure that hidden costs do not spring up, time delays do not destroy value, and continuous de-snagging is undertaken to ensure that all internal and external customers see value in their new post-implementation experience.

Technology has its downsides too. While a lot is done and will continue to be done to build firewalls around the company servers and systems, as CFO, I have always been bothered about data leakage, knowingly or unknowingly, in what can become a porous data retention system. With pen drives available in abundance across organisations, we need to worry about how much of company data moves out of the secure confines of the establishment to an unsafe environment, carried on detachable drives or copied to private e-mail IDs? For me, this has been an unaddressed bother that corporations need to think about.

Grooming Future CFOs

In my own case, I must acknowledge the role that three individuals played in shaping my career and moulding me into the manager that eventually I grew to be. The first is the late Daljit Sabikhi who was the Joint Managing Director & CFO of Tata Global Beverages and instrumental in recruiting me in 1982. I have vivid memories of my forty minute interview with Daljit Sabikhi which towards the end included a discussion on, *Herman Wouk,* whose book *War and Remembrance* I had just finished reading. Daljit was a very sharp and astute CFO. I recall him to be rather tall, slim, with sharp features and with a bit of a twang in his voice. His grasp of the business was amazing and that enabled him to take a measured view on resource allocation and ask the right questions on production, operations and sales while reviewing the company's performance. Being a man of few words, Daljit Sabikhi had no time for inefficiency or sloppiness and thus all those around him were invariably on their toes.

I recall that in 1986, I got my first promotion with an elevation from Assistant Manager to Deputy Manager. Notwithstanding my belief that the letter should have come a year earlier, I thought it would be appropriate on my part to hop across to Daljit Sabikhi's office and thank him for approving my promotion. When I tiptoed into his office, it just so happened that Daljit Sabikhi's wife Madhu had dropped by and was seated on the visitor's sofa across his table. Anyway, since I was already committed to saying my piece, I went through the motion expecting a smile in return, and perhaps, a handshake as well if I got lucky. However, what I got was neither a smile nor a handshake, but the comment from the great man stating 'you are cruising mechanically without application of mind!' That was Daljit Sabikhi's own unique way of nudging me to raise the bar and not get into complacency. In due course, Daljit Sabikhi moved on to become the Executive Vice Chairman of Rallis Ltd, a position that he held up to his untimely demise. From him I learnt the importance of attention to the minutest detail, having observed him during his preparation for board meetings or meetings with Darbari Seth, the Chairman during those days.

The second important lesson I learnt from Daljit was the importance of maintaining archives of historical data with the recognition of the fact and that at any point in time, there is only one correct number that reflects transactional facts and one should know where that information resides.

The second person I owe a lot to is Noshir Soonawala who was kind enough to offer me the CFO position in Tata Global Beverages in 2000 after the Tetley acquisition had been successfully closed. A thorough gentleman and ever so soft-spoken, from this great mind I learnt the fine art of efficient resource mobilisation and deployment. More importantly, I learnt from him the importance to always evaluate the impact on shareholders of investment decisions that we recommend or take, maintaining a fine balance between aggression and caution. Noshir Soonawala, while now having retired from any active corporate position, continues to be a Trustee with the Tata Trusts. In my view, he is, without a doubt, one of the finest brains in finance in this country.

Notwithstanding his stature, not just within the House of Tatas, but across the corporate world in India itself, Noshir Soonawala always chose to maintain a low profile, is ever so soft-spoken and not once did I ever see him ruffled. In the course of my career, whenever I did knock on his door for guidance, I came out with a solution and some very sound advice. Besides being a wizard on financial matters, Noshir Soonawala has a keen eye for art and antiques.

The third, but not the least, I owe a lot to Krishna Kumar who invariably gave me the freedom to do what I believed is good for the organisation, and from him I learnt the importance of understanding the front-end of the business in order to be an effective CFO. The importance of making decisions from the perspective of the product and services an organisation has on offer, its employees and its customers were the hallmarks of Krishna Kumar's management style.

It's the knowledge that I acquired from these three industry stalwarts that made me the professional that I am.

It is thus my belief that as leaders, CFOs must devote time and energy to identify talent within the functional domain, expose them to varying facets of the business and groom them to be future CFOs. When I reflect back on my own career, I feel relieved to note that a dozen-odd colleagues, who worked for me over the last decade and a half, across Tata Global Beverages and Indian Hotels, moved on to become CFOs of several Tata Group companies and others moved on beyond the Group and are now CFOs of significant businesses elsewhere.

Perhaps, there were some things that I did right, after all.

Is everybody in?

Is everybody in?

Is everybody in?

Let the ceremony begin.

– The Doors –

Song: Awake. **Album:** An American Prayer.
Record label: Elektra Records/Asylum Records.

The Board Room

Imagine

Over the years, with the ever-increasing focus on good corporate governance, compliance, transparency, appropriate disclosures and so on, legislation around the world, as also in India, has been progressively amended to specify and regulate the constitution and conduct of company boards. A combination of guidelines prescribed in the Companies Act 2013 along with regulations as prescribed by the Stock Exchanges and SEBI endeavour to put in place an environment that delivers consistently high standards of corporate conduct and the board's oversight of company affairs.

In a classic textbook model, assuming that the Chairman of the Board holds a non-executive position, the dynamics of the board are significantly influenced by the Chairman of the Board, who then controls and strikes a balance in the equation between the CEO and the independent directors. Such a 'control and balance' is essential in order to ensure that no individual director hijacks an agenda item and nudges the conversation at a tangent to the agenda, that everybody is heard, questions and concerns raised by the board members are addressed by the CEO and his management team and only thereafter, based upon a consensus, are agenda items approved and minutes recorded suitably.

There are a variety of expectations from the boards, their role, responsibilities, authority and deliverables. There is the most obvious role play, which includes, among other things, facilitation of company strategy, balancing long-term with short-term funds, capital allocation, ensuring the organisation is a good corporate citizen, aligning company operations to best practices, and so on. These and some similar practices are fairly well understood and give comfort to investors and other stakeholders that there is a body of individuals, that sits above management, and ensures that the interest of all stakeholders is protected, while business is being run. Effectively, boards play an intervening role and form a bridge between the capital markets, the promoters and the management. The process, if democratic enough, is meant to meet the end objectives.

Despite rather stringent regulations, which are not difficult to comprehend and an overwhelming desire among all stakeholders to ensure the highest standards of ethical conduct by an organisation, things often go wrong, and terribly so. In recent years, in the Indian corporate sector itself, the failure of Kingfisher Airlines and Satyam are illustrations of failure of the respective boards of these organisations in guiding them through the straight and narrow path. On another note, Leela Hotels finds itself in a state of financial comatose, which could have been avoided if its board had chosen to intervene early enough to avoid the company slipping into a debt trap.

In recent months, a new Pandora's box opened up with independent directors questioning the wisdom and recommendations of the principal shareholders/promoters over the latter's recommendation for a replacement of a company director. In this case, a whole new meaning to 'independence' was connoted.

This opens up a very interesting debate on what is "independence' for an independent director? Is it the right and authority to be 'independent' of management to review, critique, opine, comment upon and take a view on the affairs of the company, with no bias? Does this 'independence' even stretch beyond that and into a role that offers a view of the conduct of the principal shareholder, whose representative the independent director is to begin with? Further, in a situation where a group of independent directors has a point of view that is in conflict with the principal shareholder of the company, what happens to the organisation itself? How does the CEO then run the business, with a divided board and how does he secure a variety of shareholders approvals that are required in an ongoing manner for critical business matters such as capital raising, M&A, divestments, business restructuring, and such activities?

The key point here really is that there are no clear answers to all of this as the last thing one wants to do is to indulge in hasty generalisation.

The complexities that the boards need to deal with are immense and the responsibilities on the shoulders of the directors, individually and collectively, are onerous. Notwithstanding all this, the character and conduct of boards vary across listed companies, unlisted companies, and subsidiaries and joint venture companies of the foregoing. While the regulatory and governance protocol for Indian corporates is fairly well enumerated and articulated in the relevant legislation, the same does not necessarily apply to such companies' subsidiaries and joint ventures in overseas markets, which are governed by the offshore jurisdictions, as the case might be.

All this leads to a possible conclusion that the success of a meaningful board is substantially dependent upon self-driven desire to comply and deliver in the minds of the individual directors and less by endless regulations. If that is the case, how do we ensure that we have business oversight by meaningful boards consistently and sustainably?

To my mind, we can strive towards putting in place empowered and enlightened boards that get the job done by following a four-step process. The first and foremost discipline is in the constitution of the board itself. The second is how we facilitate the conduct of board affairs through its various subcommittees. Some are now mandatory and others, if at all, by choice. The third is clarity on the independence of the board and along with it, the clear and well-defined accountability of board members, individually and collectively as a body. Finally, if we get the first three elements right, which we need to as the stakes are just too high, we need to ensure that the boards are effective in doing what they have been entrusted to discharge.

Board Composition

The importance of minute scrutiny, evaluation and assessment of candidates before the individual being invited on to a board cannot be overstated. Prevalent legislation governs the size of the board, its mix of whole time directors, non-independent non-executive directors and after that, the independent directors. The legislation also has guidelines on gender diversity within the boardroom and a mandatory representation of independent directors in various board subcommittees. Above all this, new legislation has been brought into place to restrict the maximum undisturbed tenure of any individual director on a board and also limit the number of companies that an individual can be on the board of. All of this is undertaken with good intentions and lays down a clear intent and specifies the end goal. However, it is for the lead shareholders, who exercise the privilege and right to nominate individuals onto the board of a company to display the required care, caution and consideration in the selection process.

People get nominated onto the boards of companies for a variety of reasons, which include—a right from owning a controlling stake, a right bestowed through a shareholders agreement, by virtue of employment with the organisation, nominees of significant lenders or institutional investors and finally independent directors get invited onto the board by its Chairman.

When we look at promoter directors, their desire to ensure fair representation on the board is understandable, more so if ownership goes hand in hand with management control of the business. Professionally managed large groups are most often in a position to co-opt professional managers onto boards to fill in the 'promoter's quota' of board seats, and to that extent, they are in a position of advantage over family-run businesses where the board often gets inundated with a multitude of family members.

I am aware of a small sized listed company where the majority stake was controlled by a business family. Notwithstanding safe 'control' over the business through ownership and the right to appoint the CEO and the CFO, the family patriarch co-opted as many as five family members onto the board. This compelled the joint venture partner to co-opt his own nominees and by the time all this was balanced with the induction of independent directors, we had in the making a pretty dysfunctional board as there were just too many people in the room.

The fundamental issue here really is that a board is meant to be a body composed of visible and quantifiable skill sets, which as a combination safeguards the interest of all stakeholders. Thus, the constitution of a board must have the requisite skills regarding technical knowledge, sector knowledge, financial acumen, knowledge of regulations and enough experience in all these aspects. Board positions are not meant to be a reward nor are they meant to gratify business associates. The key criteria ought to be solely and singularly 'skill and independence,' which needs to be brought to the table.

While most listed company boards ensure that they get eminent and experienced professionals as independent directors, through which there is an adequate pool of knowledge in the room on matters relating to finance, regulations, marketing, manufacture, M&A and so on, there is in my opinion now a case to have an industry veteran on to the board as an independent director.

There is a gap in board knowledge that needs to be bridged such that they are in a position to question and challenge management on sector trends, market share, margins and quality of profits. Boards often go wrong and suboptimal proposals get approved because some board members did not get a grip of the implications of what was being proposed and the right questions were not asked for lack of knowledge of the sector itself.

Asking any number of questions, even if they seem to be rather basic, is the prerogative of board members and they need not shy away from the same. The trick is not to allow the CEO to overwhelm you with his knowledge of the business and thereby coerce the board into submission, subtly or otherwise.

With time, the complexities surrounding business, the external environment, the ever-changing regulations and disruption in the markets call for a skill set needed to run a business which is very different to what it was in the past. Gone are the days where merely functional speciality, sector knowledge and experience were a combination considered to be adequate to qualify for consideration for a board nomination. Times have changed and with that so have the minimal skill sets necessary to run businesses successfully. In the past undergraduates and diploma holders could be successful leaders. With markets being ever so combative, functional skills and experience need to be backed up by high-quality educational background, the need for which is fundamental. Knowledge does not guarantee that an individual will become a good manager, but it does no harm. Lack of knowledge can, however, be a serious deterrent in today's times as it hinders awareness and lack of awareness invariably leads to dysfunctional perceptions and conclusions.

It's helpful to ensure that the board constitution comprises of non-whole time directors who have between themselves the appropriate experience, skill set and gravitas to ask meaningful questions of the management. This is possible, without the director worrying about asking something that might be perceived to be rather basic or not relevant and can be avoided by investing time to go through an orientation, and investing time to understand the sector and after that the organisation itself.

It is safe to assume that individuals normally get invited to the boards of companies because of their past success and track record elsewhere and across a cross-section of businesses. This normally enables a very good understanding of the group on matters covering

156

macroeconomics, geopolitical, regulatory, and high-level strategy, and so on. These are often common strengths across boards.

Where boards at times falter is in their lack of understanding of the pillars that really drive a particular business and more importantly, if the business falters and the CEO is struggling to guide him towards a turnaround plan. This implies that the board members must have the inherent knowledge of the sector to ask for a drill down on what went wrong and why, how come the management was caught blindsided, what we are doing about it and thus review and approve the damage control and course correction strategy.

If sector knowledge is not available among the independent directors, the risk for the organisation is that the directors will tag along with the CEO and his plan as they do not know what to question and challenge. Difficult questions can be asked when they are backed up by options and specific suggestions.

Board Committees

Boards are successful if each director is not just perceived but seen to be on a level playing field along with the rest. This implies that no individual director should either by design or otherwise be seen to be 'more equal than the others.' The last thing that an organisation needs is any disharmony in the board and factionalism. Thus, in a perfect world, boards need to collectively and jointly be accountable as also empowered to oversee the affairs of the organisation.

Having said so, the law now mandates the formation of certain board subcommittees that are entrusted with the specific responsibility of reviewing and signing off on select matters, for subsequent review and approval by the full board based upon the recommendation of the board subcommittee. Typically, the Audit Committee, the Nominations and Remunerations Committee and the Investors Grievance Redressal Committees have mandated board subcommittees.

Often, organisations have an Executive Committee of the Board that is entrusted to review strategic issues before they come to the full board and there can be any number of board subcommittees, for one-off matters or other matters based upon business needs. The key issue here really is how we co-opt directors onto a board subcommittee, the mandate of such a committee and its deliverables.

Audit Committee

As the erstwhile Executive Director and CFO of Indian Hotels, I had the great fortune of having industry veterans of the stature of Keki Dadiseth, former Chairman of Hindustan Unilever and Deepak Parekh, Chairman of HDFC on our Audit Committee, with Keki Dadiseth chairing the same. Soon after Keki Dadiseth took over as the Chairman of the Audit Committee, he decided to set up a regular pre-Audit Committee discussion on the quarterly financial results and any outstanding points as the case may be with the audit partners and me. Such a review by the Chairman of the Audit Committee, before each formal Audit Committee meetings, gave him the luxury of time to delve into the business, the numbers, the issues, risks and mitigation strategy and so on. In quick time, Keki had a remarkable grip over the affairs of the company and all its complexities and the audit partners had the comfort that they could speak their minds, be heard and that the board was seized of matters that needed its specific attention. As CFO, I was very comfortable with the process as it kept my team on its toes and this detailed process gave me comfort that all is well and that the auditors have specifically drawn my attention to matters that I need to personally address or get done.

Separately, Deepak Parekh would occasionally seek a one-to-one meeting between the Audit Committee and the Audit Partners, without management being present. This helped reinforce the independence of the auditors in the mind of the Audit Committee and thus the board. As onerous as the task of the Audit Committees is in today's highly regulated environment, the good news is that the mandate, authority and accountability of such committees is unambiguous.

Investors Grievance Redressal Committee

In the case of some other board activities, undertaken through board subcommittees, the roles are changing and need to be redefined. One such case is the need to redefine the scope and role of the Investors Grievance Redressal committee of the board. While these are mandated committees, the scope of their role needs a quick redefinition to make this subcommittee effective and a source of relevant and important feedback flowing back to the boards. In the old days, these subcommittees had been set up to look into investor complaints about non-receipt of dividends, share transfers, non-receipt of the company's Annual Report, encashment of Fixed Deposits, and the like.

With time, all the aforementioned issues have by and large come to rest as they are now dealt with online, with minimal management intervention. The focus of this committee now needs to shift to a higher plain and to really relevant issues. Boards seldom focus on company shareholding, a mix of shareholding amongst non-promoter investors, institutional investors, foreign institutional investors, and the like. It is thus important for this board subcommittee to dig into changes in shareholding and to understand from the CFO—who is selling, who is buying and why, as also its implications on the market capitalisation.

In the Indian capital market environment, share price sentiments are nowadays influenced by the behaviour of domestic institutional investors as also the foreign institutional investors as this group is the one that is active in the stock market. The retail investors are too small in volume and to state the obvious, the promoters and government shareholding is illiquid.

It's time for board subcommittees to spend time with the CFO to better understand the dynamic of what is in play here and the relevance of the mix of significant investors. To facilitate an understanding of all this, the directors need to get a quarterly debrief on investors and research analysts met by the CFO and management, look at some significant research reports published about the company and understand any material concern or criticism being voiced and management response to the same.

An ongoing and transparent communication between management and the investor and analyst community is now a way of life and in the recent past stock exchanges have made it obligatory on the part of management to regularly disclose to them the particulars of investors and analysts met by the management along with the summary of subject matter discussed. This protocol is required to ensure that all company related information percolates evenly across the external stakeholders and that it is out in the public domain concurrently, which is all the more reason for the board to get a better grip on all this.

In recent times, there is a compulsion for management to seek prior and specific board and shareholders' approval for a variety of business matters, which in the past was not the case. This protocol now encompasses even the material subsidiary companies of the listed holding company. Such proposals need to go to the shareholders for prior approval that can be secured often through a postal ballot and for certain specified purposes a shareholders' extraordinary general meeting is required to be called for. On such matters, the board needs to get a grip on the trends of shareholders who have voted against the management proposal and understand their disconnect with the management for the same.

Linked to this is the emerging investor advisory firms, which have sprung up of late and play the role of a vigilante on behalf of their subscriber members. In today's times, it is important for management to engage with these firms and ensure that whatever is in the public domain is clearly articulated and explained to the advisory firms, such that they can write their reports based upon full knowledge and facts. Because the stakes are high and organisational reputation can be tarnished in the event of a shareholder's ballot not sailing through, this board subcommittee needs to now start spending the time to better understand the dynamics of how the various players in the stock market operate and influence the organisation.

The recent spat between the Infosys board, its former CEO and the company's promotors is a good illustration of a board caught blindsided and thus ill-prepared to deal with the emotions and sentiments of its significant shareholders. The issue really is not about who or what is right. It's about managing public perceptions as well.

Finally, management often meets significant investors, fund managers, analysts and the like. It is advisable for the board subcommittee to seek a detailed brief on content shared, feedback received, any concerns about company strategy that's been made public, and such factors.

Risk Mitigation Committee

Often, an Audit Committee also doubles up to cover Risk Assessment and management's mitigation plan thereof. The key point that board members need to bear in mind is that elements of sector risk keep changing with varying intensity thereof. The external environmental risks covering currency, money markets, geopolitical factors, and so on witness seismic shifts and short notice and the directors need to ensure that management does not take their eyes off the ball.

Finally, boards need to be aware of the company's credit rating that directly influences the cost of debt, of any negative comments in the rating agency's report, and also be aware of any rating downgrade risks. These are relevant concern areas and seldom get discussed in boardrooms.

Remunerations and Nominations Committee

The Remunerations and Nominations Committee of the Board plays a critical role screening whole time directors as also independent directors prior to their induction onto the board, performance evaluation and compensation for whole time directors, performance review and annual compensation of key managerial personnel and of late, the Chairman of this committee can be requested to facilitate evaluation of the boards' own performance, and so on. It is important for the organisation, as also for the shareholders, to ensure that this committee exercises independent judgement in the job at hand and that it is not overtly influenced by the CEO's recommendation of year-end compensation increases and performance bonuses. This committee needs to work independently of the CEO.

Before we get into compensation, the committee needs to first and foremost spell out the key performance matrices that shall be taken into consideration to evaluate a CEO's performance. I would recommend the following six criteria be used to evaluate a CEO's annual performance:

- Action taken to address and resolve legacy problems that the CEO may have inherited from his predecessor. Once the incumbent occupies the corner room, there is no escape from this as very often significant capital is blocked in underperforming assets that need a time-bound address.

- Improvement in margins, across the core business, isolating non-operational credits.

- Efficiency in executing greenfield projects, costs, timelines and ROI from new capital deployed.

- Customer satisfaction, increase in key customer contribution and review of lost business.

- People policy, building bench strength, talent attraction and retention skills and the CEO's focus on training.

- Finally, the CEO needs to be evaluated on how he has driven a culture of innovation across the organisation to create differentiation and an edge through new products, processes, new technology, and such factors.

In effect, a combination of measurement criteria covering Balance Sheet focus and Profit and Loss or P&L focus, with an eye on the future can be a winning formula for the business. Needless to say, a significant percentage of the annual compensation has to be linked to the annual organisational goals and within that the individual's contribution. The last thing that the committee should accept is a fixed guaranteed compensation for anybody in the senior leadership of the organisation.

There is an organisation that for reasons best known to it, recruited a new CEO with a guaranteed annual performance bonus, unlinked to organisational goals and company performance. At the year-end, the CEO was reviewing the performance of his direct reports and realised that based upon the pre-agreed criteria, many of his direct reports would fall 20 percent short of their eligible annual bonus as many key organisational goals had fallen short. Clearly, the CEO felt uncomfortable collecting his own full bonus, while his team fell short. So the story goes that the CEO recalibrated the goals for his team to ensure that they all got their maximum bonuses and he would not stand out like a sore thumb.

It was a disaster for the organisation to say the least and made a farce of the entire process. This led to a domino effect across the organisation with the rank and file also earning a performance bonus in excess of what they would have earned linked to actual goals achieved. In effect, besides the avoidable incremental costs borne by the company, the short-sightedness of the leadership team lowered the performance bar of the organisation—irreversible damage.

The effectiveness and empowerment of the Remuneration and Nominations Committee can be evaluated on how empowered does this committee feel to be in a position to alter or veto a recommendation based upon a measured view! How often does this really happen, if at all?

Executive Committee

Some organisations have an Executive Committee comprising of select board members, with such a committee mandated to focus on strategic issues, as a small group, before the same being formally tabled to the full board. Such committees have met with a mixed response from the point of view of effectiveness, as often, directors that were not included felt isolated. This goes back to my earlier point of drawing a distinction between a board committee formed for a specific and limited objective as against a board committee formed with a wide and ambiguous mandate. The latter does not work efficiently as in the organisational interest, all board members need to be on a level playing field.

Board Accountability and Independence

The accountability of the board can be enabled if as the first step, we can ensure the board's independence vis-a-vis the CEO and the management. After all, it's the board's responsibility to ensure that capital is deployed to grow the business intelligently, investments yield the desired threshold returns, problems are pre-empted and addressed, opportunities in the market are created and seized, and thereby the organisation adds value for its stakeholders.

Sector Knowledge

Being independent of management is easier said than done. True independence begins with the ability of every board member being knowledgeable about the sector and reasonably well versed with the ever-changing sector-specific dynamics that impact business, either favourably or vice versa. To facilitate the foregoing, boards need to be able to tap into industry knowledge that is credible and independent of what management tables.

In Indian Hotels, when Ratan Tata was the Chairman of the company, we used to periodically present to the board — a comparison of the Taj's performance across its portfolio in Mumbai and Delhi as compared to the global peer group in markets such as Bangkok, Singapore and Hong Kong. The data was subscribed to from reputed research firms that aggregated such information across its subscribing members and provided analytics, across markets, while shielding the identity of specific competitive sets. Such diagnostics was supplemented by the company's own performance as compared to its domestic peers as well. This exercise provided the board with a good view of the Taj's strengths, across parameters along with the visibility of variables where the Taj was at a competitive disadvantage and needed to do something about it.

Orientation Program

A well-structured orientation program is a must for all incoming new independent directors. Directors themselves must not hesitate to seek such a well-meaning introduction to the organisation that they are getting associated with, but more importantly, it can help new inductees hit the turf running. Such orientation programmes should cover, inter alia, industry background, competitive set, recent company performance trends, products, brands, customers and key issues under address.

Board Agenda

Boards need to be vocal about what they need to see, how and thus what they would like to be covered in the agenda. This would ensure that there is no inadvertent dilution in information flow and management focuses on what the board asks for along with what the management itself wishes to table to the board. This calls for a fine balance in putting together of board agendas, balancing the requirements and priorities of management as also the independent directors on the board.

The success of this process, which is rather fundamental in nature lies in the CEO not feeling insecure or overwhelmed by demands from the board as the CEO needs to understand and appreciate that the board is accountable for the CEO's actions and the consequences thereof.

Self-Evaluation

Of late, legislation has mandated that boards partake in a self-evaluation of their individual effectiveness and contribution in board deliberations. While this is a move in the right direction, these are early days for this process to mature and be a facilitator to improve the dynamics of a board's working. The ultimate test of this process would lie in a board's ability and willingness to ask a director to step down on account of indifferent feedback from the peers. That would be real independence, albeit not fraught with controversies, and in reality difficult to implement.

Board Effectiveness

As discussed earlier, the prerequisite to ensuring optimal effectiveness of company boards commences with the constitution of the board itself, the boards functioning, collectively and through its various subcommittees, and recognition amongst the board members themselves of their individual and collective accountability towards all stakeholders.

While it's easy and fashionable to talk of accountability, rarely do we see a company board being held responsible for significant failure or lapses of an organisation that leads to the erosion of shareholder value. CEOs are often changed when they do not deliver or something goes dramatically wrong within an organisation; there needs to be a mechanism that enables a review of the board constitution itself in such situations.

Board Responsibility

Directors now need to understand and accept that they are individually and collectively responsible for the organisation and the outcome of significant board decisions. When things go well, which hopefully is usually the case, the credit goes to all—the management team as also the company board. Alternately, when the house collapses, it has to be a collective responsibility as well. Board members, thus need to understand that, if satisfied, they need to fully endorse each individual board decision.

Conversely, if they specifically voice a concern and opinion against any matter that triggers discomfort in their minds, they need to seek explanations and answers from the management to each individual's satisfaction. Being politically correct is not what they are there for and there is thus no mid-path towards acceptable board accountability. The same applies to board decisions. Once an individual director votes in favour of an agenda item, he is fully committed. There is no scope for qualitative approvals. It is best that the collective board ensures that.

Schedule of Authority

Effective company board function can be facilitated with a clear policy agreed to between the board and the management on what must come to the board for prior review and approval, authority that the board delegates to the CEO and the CFO to enable the day-to-day running of the business, approval for further down the line delegated authority, across businesses and cross-functional, such that there is abundant clarity amongst all on decision-making empowerment. Often, organisations document such a policy through a Schedule of Authority that captures the intent.

The Companies Act 2013 itself lays down a variety of criteria that, perforce, need a prior and specific board or shareholders' approval. Notwithstanding the same, a business cannot be over regulated nor can regulations capture all potential scenarios on decisions and transactions that may need prior board approval. The solutions, thus, lie in an elegant capture and understanding of the 'spirit of the intent' that would ensure the appropriate governance protocol is in place, covering nature of transactions and others through a value materiality threshold. The spirit of intent is really the guiding factor here. To illustrate, it's now mandated that recruitment of all key managerial personnel and their compensation needs to be prior approved by the Remuneration and Nominations Committee of the Board. This is to ensure that the appropriate talent is in place to run the business efficiently, that such talent is compensated in line with the market or industry practice, and so on. If that be the case, the board would presumably not expect the management to recruit an executive, below the level of a key managerial person, on compensation terms that are not aligned to market and the cost of the position is very material. Similarly, the board would not expect the management to change benefit policies across the organisation in a manner that exposes the organisation to recurring costs in perpetuity.

The Content of Board Agenda

Businesses run into the ground very often as the management and the boards did not read the smoke signals right or just did not see the signals at all. Thus, it is helpful or rather necessary for the board to know and be clear about what they need to see when reviewing organisational performance, what criteria to review, and really be in a position to judge objectively where the business has done well, where not so, based upon an understanding of competitive data and draw their own conclusions as against over-relying on the CEO presentation and his own perspective of how the business is doing.

This calls for an ability on the part of the board to be able to sift through and zero in on the underperforming parts of the business, underutilised assets, a well-performing subsect of the business and the rest that needs to measure up to potential. The board should thus know what information to ask for. This comes with knowledge and a rolled-up sleeves approach.

While success in running businesses in the past is no guarantee to assure ongoing success in the boardroom and a measurable contribution towards the company affairs, it helps. It is desirable that board members are reasonably active in their chosen fields, which would mean that their knowledge of their chosen fields would also be current and thus relevant to the organisation they serve.

Board agendas need to be decluttered and presented in a style and format that invites the reader's attention to the key issues that need his attention. Many organisations thus present board agenda items in four well-defined subsects covering routine items, company performance and operating matters, investment decisions, regulatory and compliance matters. Because of the compulsion to have a board meeting for the adoption and publication of quarterly audited financial results, four meetings perforce get earmarked for quarterly results. Another would be dedicated for review and approval of annual business plans. One meeting is required on strategy formulation, review of implementation and course correction matters and yet another would be needed for investments, restructuring, and any other related matters that need board attention. In the given scenario, the board would need to convene at least eight times a year.

Board agenda items need to be well drafted, be crisp, provide relevant details and not be unduly bulky. Visually appealing texts or PowerPoint presentations is an important necessity to ensure that you catch the attention of the reader in the first moment itself. I have always believed that inelegant and tardy presentations most certainly dilute the absorption of the content in the minds of the reader as the attention span breaks. PowerPoint presentations are all about making 'powerful points' by using the bullet points on a slide as a cue. It is lethal to go for an overkill, pad up data, text, visuals on a slide as it can lead to a disaster. The important thing is not to talk about or inform the board what it already knows.

There is a CEO of a company who is known for making a hundred slide presentations to his board each quarter, on company results, with each slide extremely heavy with pictures, logos, tables, and so on. The flow and structure of his presentation did not change for years and the board was too polite to ask him to edit it down to what was relevant information. Boards need to be smart about this and insist on a crisp and to-the-point presentations. The idea is that a presentation is used merely as a cue sheet by the presenter, who then is expected to speak extempore and not meander through a pre-prepared script.

Board Offsite

Informal off sites, once in a while is a good way for the board to spend some fully focused quality time on company matters, take the opportunity to interact with the second rung of leadership, the functional heads and others, who otherwise do not get invited into board meetings. This is helpful as it is important for board members to be able to access the company's senior leadership without being supervised by the CEO and get a perspective of what is going on in the sector and within the organisation from a wider group.

Ongoing Updates on Regulatory Changes

Boards need to spend some quality time to review the ever-changing regulatory environment and the impact it has on the sector and the organisations. While it is a given that board members would be familiar with such moving sands by virtue of their positions elsewhere, the issue really is that regulatory changes impact sectors, and often organisations within a sector in varying manners. The Indian corporate world migrated to the IND-AS accounting standards in 2016 and with that, the profitability matrix and Balance Sheets changed permanently.

Companies that have significant investment overseas, through wholly-owned subsidiaries are grappling with Transfer Pricing issues with the exchequer, further tax changes have been brought about through the introduction of Place of Effective Management, which widens the tax net for the authorities to cover overseas subsidiaries and joint ventures of Indian corporates if the operations of the former are overseen out of India. This new legislation will have far-reaching ramifications, the impact of which has as yet not been measured.

In this regard, while consolidation of financials is now mandatory in India, it is more for compliance with SEBI and the Stock Exchange guidelines. Unlike elsewhere in the world, tax consolidation is as yet not permitted in India. Finally, with the recent introduction of the Goods and Services Tax the pricing of goods and services in the hands of the end consumers have dramatically changed. These are all far-reaching changes in the external environment and boards need to ensure that they are well versed with the implications thereof.

Capital Allocation

Capital allocation is among one of the most important tasks placed before the board. Seldom do we see an investment opportunity tabled to the board that does not promise a positive Economic Value Add, an internal rate of return well above the cost of capital, risk mitigation backup plans and thus a compelling case from the management for approval to pursue the project.

The key issue here really is how engaged boards are on monitoring the progress of investment decisions once management has secured approvals for the same. All project viability sensitivity analysis can be rendered meaningless on account of time delays in execution and cost overruns in Greenfield projects. Capital availability is not infinite and the board needs to take a view on when a bird in the hand can be let off because the two in the bush are worth a pursuit. Questions that the board needs to ask are—do we need to do this at all? Why do we need to spend this much? Can it be done for less? Is the execution timeline realistic and are the economic returns indicated achievable?

A good way to get a grip on all this is to, as a discipline, periodically review the performance of new assets versus the pre-investment assumptions that were tabled to the board. Such a diagnostic will invariably throw up some interesting insights.

The hospitality sector, around the world, is very capital intensive and suffers from a long gestation period. The business is seasonal and impacted by cyclicality like all other sectors. While capital calls will be made by management when pursuing organic and inorganic growth opportunities, in this business, boards need to keep an eye on ensuring that management does not take its eye off the ball while ensuring good health of existing assets.

Ongoing investments back in the business are required to ensure that operating assets are invariably kept fresh to extend the life thereof. This is necessary, even at the cost of margin erosion and must be necessarily undertaken during economic downturns. When assets do come up for renovation, boards must have a view on how much the organisation can or should invest across revenue-generating areas and why. The fact of the matter is design and interiors are extremely subjective and strongly influenced subconsciously by personal likes and dislikes. Such subjectivity can influence an oscillation in costs that are unrelated to the willingness of the customer to pay a premium for the facility, once it is back in the market after renovation. It is at this stage that the board needs to ask the relevant questions.

Company Strategy

Boards focus a lot on facilitating company strategy on growth, new products, new markets, all combined to enable the organisation to retain its competitive edge, protect and enhance margins and thus continue to remain relevant in the market. Having said this, my firm belief is that boards need to play a calming role here and strike the much-needed balance between pushing the management to expand the business and ensuring long-term sustainable margin enhancement.

The fundamental issue here is that the boards themselves need to challenge the myth that all growth will eventually translate into enhanced profitability. Nothing is farther from the truth. I have mentioned elsewhere in this book that unknowingly, organisations continue to make suboptimal investments and underperforming assets get buried under those that perform. To add to the organisation's woes, we end up throwing more and more money behind ailing assets, often at the cost of the anchor assets.

For this reason, it is important that boards need to be well informed about where margins are accruing for the organisation and where there is value erosion. In cases of value erosion, boards must demand a time-bound, sector-specific turnaround plan that needs to be monitored. Running a business calls for a heart of steel and the ability to take measured risks. If we are not willing to take measured risks, we might as well put our money in bank deposits. So risk-taking is a given, while running a business.

What is needed and which often does not receive the required focus from boards is a strategy to fix what is broken in a time-bound manner. Organisations are often reluctant to shut down a failed business, which cannot be turned around despite best efforts, and there can be any number

173

of reasons for the same. In such cases, the solution lies in accepting the failure on the chin and moving on. Ensuring a course correction in a time-bound manner is a priority that boards need to focus on as eventually they need to ensure a harmonised balance between management desire and shareholders' expectations. Shareholders are patient and can be forgiving, but they too expect time-bound remedial action.

A good way to ensure that the board is fully engaged, aware, knowledgeable, and asks the relevant questions is to ensure that the discussion and debates on the board agenda items are invariably well drafted and capture the varying views, opinions and explanations submitted before a consensus and decision is taken.

In the pursuit of profitable growth, market share and sector leadership, measured risks need to be taken to achieve the organisation's long-term strategic objectives. Often, such investment decisions deliver the desired results, but at times they don't. In such cases, there is no shame in management accepting that some strategic calls and investments did not deliver the required results and yield to investors. It's alright, provided management acknowledges it and makes a quick enough course correction. Inertia is not pardonable nor is it fair to shareholders.

In conclusion, under the new order, the accountability of the CEOs, CFOs and that of the company boards are increasingly intertwined. Further, the roles and responsibilities of each have dramatically changed and that needs to be recognised. The management leadership and the company boards need to be fully aligned. Such an alignment will enable guiding the company to achieve its strategic objectives, execute its long-term plans and in the process, keep adding value for its shareholders and other stakeholders.

As I reflect over my experiences in the corporate world, I am reminded of John Lennon's memorable quote:

"Life is what happens to you when you're busy making other plans."

It's so true for business as well!

We should change our way of thought

More if we do not, the way ahead

Is dangerously fraught

And if we did the things we all know to be right

Left would be the childish fears

Of dangers in the night

– Moody Blues –

Song: Nothing Changes. **Album:** Strange Times. **Record label:** Universal Records.

Acknowledgements

I have many people to thank, who have in the course of writing this book provided me with invaluable critique, insights and suggestions on the manuscript, as its various versions developed. Parvathi Venkatraman reviewed the first draft of the manuscript and guided me on the structure and layout of the narrative as would be expected by the publishing world.

As a first-time writer, I felt it would be helpful to get an independent critique from some friends on the general flow of the narrative as it unfurled, while my own thoughts continued to crystallise. Sunil Sherole, Ramnath Krishnan and Rina Sen Goel, had a look at the first draft of the manuscript and provided me with a critique on what they thought of the structure and flow of the narrative as it was developing. I am grateful to all three for their respective contribution in reviewing the manuscript and providing suggestions.

My friend Atul Sinha had a look at the manuscript at a stage when I felt it was almost ready. Atul and I go back a long way having been to school and college together. Having spent many years in the corporate world himself, Atul's suggestions went a long way in helping me finish the manuscript and bring matters to a finality.

Raghav Kapur, my son-in-law, was the last person to have a look at the manuscript just before I handed it over to the publisher for the formal round of editing and review. Raghav's observations and suggestions on the narrative were invaluable.

Over the many months that I took to write the book and work on its numerous edits, my wife Vaishali continued to be supportive and encouraged me all along the way, displaying the firm belief that this book has a narrative that needs to be told.

Finally, I am immensely grateful to the team at Notion Press for supporting the publication of the book and guiding me through the entire process. I am also deeply indebted to the Notion Press team that oversaw the book launch and its marketing.

This book would not have been possible without the support of all the aforementioned friends and well-wishers.

July 14, 2018

The End

References

Future Shock - Alvin Toffler

The Third Wave - Alvin Toffler

Power Shift - Alvin Toffler

Facets of 100 Years of Planting - Amita Baig and W Henderson

Fairy Dell - Thommen Kuruvilla

Beliefs, Behaviours and Results - Scott Gillis, Lee Mergy, Joe Shalleck

Boards at Work - Ram Charan

Annual Report for 2015/16 - The Indian Hotels Company Ltd

Annual Report for 2017/18 - Tata Global Beverages Ltd

Standalone Annual Report for 2016/17 - Flipkart India Private Ltd as filed with the ROC

Lyrics by the following musicians/groups have been quoted:

Moody Blues

Bob Dylan

The Doors

Pink Floyd

Crosby, Stills and Nash

George Harrison

The Eagles

J J Cale

Allman Brothers Band

John Lennon

Printed in Great Britain
by Amazon

17859517R00120